BUILDING
HISTORY
SERIES

STONEHENGE

by Wendy Mass

Lucent Books, Inc., San Diego, California

TITLES IN THE BUILDING HISTORY SERIES INCLUDE:

The Great Wall of China
The Medieval Castle
The New York Subway System
The Panama Canal
The Pyramids of Giza
The Roman Colosseum
Stonehenge

For my parents

Library of Congress Cataloging-in-Publication Data

Mass, Wendy, 1967–
     Stonehenge / by Wendy Mass.
       p.   cm. — (Building history series)
     Includes bibliographical references (p.   ) and index.
     Summary: Discusses the history, construction, and possible
purposes of Stonehenge.
     ISBN 1-56006-432-3 (lib. : alk. paper)
     1. Stonehenge (England)—Juvenile literature.   2. Wiltshire
(England)—Antiquities—Juvenile literature.   3. Megalithic
monuments—England—Wiltshire—Juvenile literature.
[1. Stonehenge (England)   2. Megalithic monuments.
3. England—Antiquities.]   I. Title.   II. Series.
DA142.M37   1998
936.2'319—dc21
                                                                97-47569
                                                                  CIP
                                                                  AC

Copyright 1998 by Lucent Books, Inc.
P.O. Box 289011, San Diego, California 92198-9011

Printed in the U.S.A.

CONTENTS

FOREWORD   4

IMPORTANT DATES IN THE BUILDING
   OF STONEHENGE   6

INTRODUCTION   8

CHAPTER ONE
   Early Stonehenge: The Building Site   11

CHAPTER TWO
   Early Stages of Construction   29

CHAPTER THREE
   Later Stages of Construction   45

CHAPTER FOUR
   What Was the Purpose of Stonehenge?   60

CHAPTER FIVE
   Destruction, Restoration, and Preservation   73

   Notes   87
   For Further Reading   89
   Works Consulted   90
   Index   91
   Picture Credits   95
   About the Author   96

FOREWORD

Throughout history, as civilizations have evolved and prospered, each has produced unique buildings and architectural styles. Combining the need for both utility and artistic expression, a society's buildings, particularly its large-scale public structures, often reflect the individual character traits that distinguish it from other societies. In a very real sense, then, buildings express a society's values and unique characteristics in tangible form. As scholar Anita Abramovitz comments in her book *People and Spaces*, "Our ways of living and thinking—our habits, needs, fear of enemies, aspirations, materialistic concerns, and religious beliefs—have influenced the kinds of spaces that we build and that later surround and include us."

That specific types and styles of structures constitute an outward expression of the spirit of an individual people or era can be seen in the diverse ways that various societies have built palaces, fortresses, tombs, churches, government buildings, sports arenas, public works, and other such monuments. The ancient Greeks, for instance, were a supremely rational people who originated Western philosophy and science, including the atomic theory and the realization that the earth is a sphere. Their public buildings, epitomized by Athens's magnificent Parthenon temple, were equally rational, emphasizing order, harmony, reason, and above all, restraint.

By contrast, the Romans, who conquered and absorbed the Greek lands, were a highly practical people preoccupied with acquiring and wielding power over others. The Romans greatly admired and readily copied elements of Greek architecture, but modified and adapted them to their own needs. "Roman genius was called into action by the enormous practical needs of a world empire," wrote historian Edith Hamilton. "Rome met them magnificently. Buildings tremendous, indomitable, amphitheaters where eighty thousand could watch a spectacle, baths where three thousand could bathe at the same time."

In medieval Europe, God heavily influenced and motivated the people, and religion permeated all aspects of society, molding people's worldviews and guiding their everyday actions. That spiritual mindset is reflected in the most important medieval structure—the Gothic cathedral—which, in a sense, was a model of heavenly cities. As scholar Anne Fremantle so ele-

4

gantly phrases it, the cathedrals were "harmonious elevations of stone and glass reaching up to heaven to seek and receive the light [of God]."

Our more secular modern age, in contrast, is driven by the realities of a global economy, advanced technology, and mass communications. Responding to the needs of international trade and the growth of cities housing millions of people, today's builders construct engineering marvels, among them towering skyscrapers of steel and glass, mammoth marine canals, and huge and elaborate rapid transit systems, all of which would have left their ancestors, even the Romans, awestruck.

In examining some of humanity's greatest edifices, Lucent Books' Building History series recognizes this close relationship between a society's historical character and its buildings. Each volume in the series begins with a historical sketch of the people who erected the edifice, exploring their major achievements as well as the beliefs, customs, and societal needs that dictated the variety, functions, and styles of their buildings. A detailed explanation of how the selected structure was conceived, designed, and built, to the extent that this information is known, makes up the majority of the volume.

Each volume in the Lucent Building History series also includes several special features that are useful tools for additional research. A chronology of important dates gives students an overview, at a glance, of the evolution and use of the structure described. Sidebars create a broader context by adding further details on some of the architects, engineers, and construction tools, materials, and methods that made each structure a reality, as well as the social, political, and/or religious leaders and movements that inspired its creation. Useful maps help the reader locate the nations, cities, streets, and individual structures mentioned in the text; and numerous diagrams and pictures illustrate tools and devices that bring to life various stages of construction. Finally, each volume contains two bibliographies, one for student research, the other listing works the author consulted in compiling the book.

Taken as a whole, these volumes, covering diverse ancient and modern structures, constitute not only a valuable research tool, but also a tribute to the human spirit, a fascinating exploration of the dreams, skills, ingenuity, and dogged determination of the great peoples who shaped history.

IMPORTANT DATES IN THE BUILDING OF STONEHENGE

2100–2000
Round barrows replace long barrows in Stonehenge IIIa; sarsens transported from Marlborough Downs.

2500–2100
Stonehenge II; bluestones transported from Wales.

3900
Robin Hood's Ball is built by early Neolithic tribes.

3300
The Great Cursus is built.

8000 B.C.
Ancient Britons build totem poles on Salisbury Plain.

B.C. 8000	7000	6000	5000	4000	3000	2000

4000
Beginning of farming in Britain.

2000–1550
Stonehenge IIIb; both types of stones used in monument.

3500
People begin burying their dead in long barrows.

3100–2700
Neolithic builders dig a circular bank and ditch on Salisbury Plain known as Stonehenge I.

2300
Woodhenge built.

Stonehenge as it appears today.

1550–1100
Stonehenge IIIc; final arrangement of stones.

250
Druids first appear in Britain.

Stonehenge is one of the most popular tourist attractions in England.

2000
A million visitors are expected at Stonehenge.

1950s–1960s
The invention of radiocarbon dating provides reliable dates for events at Stonehenge.

1136
Stonehenge first mentioned in written records.

1898
First fence is built around Stonehenge; visitors are charged admission.

| 1000 | A.D. 50 | 1200 | 1800 | 1900 | 2000 |

A.D. 61
Romans allegedly tear down part of Stonehenge.

1918
Cecil Chubb, owner of Stonehenge, donates monument to the government.

1802
First official archaeological excavations begin at Stonehenge.

1985
The Battle of the Beanfield occurs when police clash with partygoers on their way to an annual festival at Stonehenge; 420 people arrested.

1100
Stonehenge Avenue extended toward the bank of the River Avon.

 # INTRODUCTION

Stonehenge has mystified and impressed generations of visitors and scholars who travel to Salisbury Plain in Wiltshire, England, eighty miles west of London, to marvel at the wonder of this ruin. Who created this prehistoric monument? How was it built? What is its significance? These questions have kept the mystery of Stonehenge alive for thousands of years, and the combined investigative efforts of historians, geologists, engineers, archaeologists, astronomers, chemists, and philosophers have continued to uncover more questions than answers. As a keen observer declared in 1801, "The mazes of wild opinion [about Stonehenge] are more complex and intricate than the ruin."[1]

The name Stonehenge is believed to have been derived from words that mean either "circle of stones," "hanging stones," or "stone hinges." The earliest surviving written reference to the monument (then called by its Latin name *stanenges*,

An aerial view of Stonehenge in Wiltshire, England. The name Stonehenge is believed to be derived from words for "circle of stones," "hanging stones," or "stone hinges."

These massive stones were erected thousands of years ago to form Stonehenge, a daunting architectural feat that continues to awe and amaze visitors.

or *stanhenge*) was written by a Norman historian named Henry of Huntingdon. In A.D. 1130 Henry noticed how the stones form sets of doorways if viewed from certain angles: "Stanenges, where stones of wonderful size have been erected after the manner of doorways, so that doorway appears to have been raised upon doorway; and no one can conceive how such great stones have been so raised aloft, or why they were built there." [2]

SEEING THE PAST

Stonehenge, called the most photographed site in the world, draws nearly a million visitors a year, almost half of them from the United States. A British government agency called the English Heritage Foundation is the guardian of the site itself and Great Britain's National Trust owns the 1,450 acres surrounding the monument. This landscape contains the largest concentration of prehistoric burial mounds and earthworks in northwestern Europe. The structure itself is the ruin of a single building, but a building unlike any other ever built. It never had a roof, and it was in a near constant state of construction. Each phase of building spanned as long as a few hundred years, sometimes separated by brief dormant periods. Construction began as early as 3100 B.C. and continued until around 1100 B.C. The ruin that stands today, five thousand years after the first circle was dug, reveals only glimpses of its former incarnations and challenges archaeologists to determine what part of the monument was constructed at what time and by whom. Nevertheless, it is possible to piece together an image of the monument in its final stage—four concentric series of stones encircled by an embankment—although today most of the stones are missing, leaning, or lying broken on the ground.

THE FUTURE

There are almost as many legends and folktales about Stonehenge as there are stones erected there, and these stories reveal much about the cultures from which they originated. With advances in technology have come sophisticated methods of dating objects found by excavation. More accurate dating has given archaeologists a much clearer picture of the people who constructed the monument over the centuries, as well as more precise estimates of when the stones were erected and shifted around over time. Scientists are the first to admit, however, that discoveries in the future may alter their current knowledge of Stonehenge. Today, the major focus is on how to protect the stones so that future generations can safely marvel at them as well. At this, the beginning of a new millennium, scientists know more than ever before about Stonehenge, a place that guards its secrets well.

Early Stonehenge: The Building Site

Stonehenge originally comprised approximately 162 stone blocks, only half of which survive today. The ruin stands in southern England, two and a half miles west of the town of Amesbury in Wiltshire. It is eight miles north of the city of Salisbury, thirty miles north of the English Channel. The monument is located near the top of a slight slope (about 330 feet above sea level), but the ground under the stones is almost flat. Though it appears isolated, Stonehenge is actually part of an intricate network of ceremonial structures built in the region over thousands of years. It is necessary to study Stonehenge within the context of the landscape and structures around it in order to get a true sense of its place in history.

The History of the Site

Stonehenge stands amid gently rolling plains called downs; if the surrounding twentieth-century tourist facilities were to disappear it would be the only structure visible aboveground. Only a few inches beneath the soil is the softest type of calcareous rock—chalk—a porous, weak, and generally unstable building foundation. In light of this instability, archaeologists have wondered why that particular site was chosen for such an ambitious project. The entire area clearly had special importance because hundreds of burial mounds and the remains of both stone and wooden circles exist in the immediate vicinity, some of which predate Stonehenge's first stages of construction.

Scientists now have proof that the site of Stonehenge had been used for some special purpose as long ago as 8000 B.C., when improvements in climate drew prehistoric peoples to northern Europe at the end of the Ice Age. Their evidence is the recent discovery of three holes for totem poles or similar ceremonial timber structures that were uncovered while creating a parking lot for visitors to Stonehenge. The date was reached by

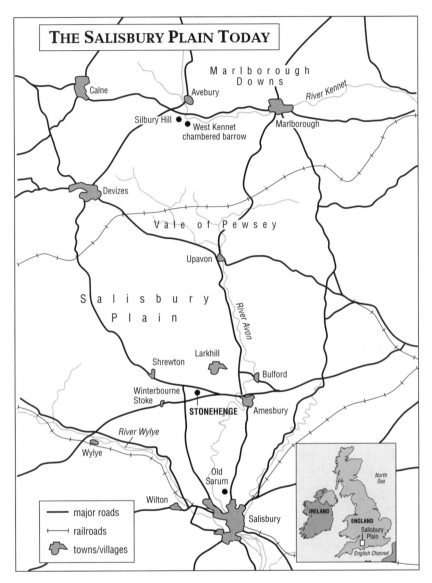

THE SALISBURY PLAIN TODAY

Marlborough Downs

Calne

Avebury

River Kennet

Silbury Hill
West Kennet
chambered barrow

Marlborough

Devizes

Vale of Pewsey

Upavon

Salisbury Plain

River Avon

Larkhill

Shrewton

Bulford

Winterbourne Stoke

STONEHENGE   Amesbury

River Wylye

Wylye

Old Sarum

Wilton

Salisbury

— major roads
railroads
towns/villages

North Sea

IRELAND

ENGLAND

Salisbury Plain

English Channel

scientifically dating pieces of charcoal and pine and a piece of burnt bone that were found in the holes.

Before 4700 B.C., the end of the Mesolithic period in England (separating the Old Stone Age from the Neolithic period) the land would have been covered with lush forests. Not until well into the Neolithic period, characterized by the use of polished stone tools, did the first builders of Stonehenge begin their work. Neolithic men cleared the forests for primitive farming, to provide grazeland for cattle, and for raising pigs. But, according to famed Stonehenge archaeologist Richard Atkinson, their efforts would not have left the plains as bare and treeless as they are today. Rather, the terrain would instead be "broken by at least occasional thickets of thorn, juniper, and gorse, and possibly by scattered but isolated trees."[3]

Because there are no written records of life back then, nor signs of settlements in the immediate area (which would have left more clues for archaeologists to piece together a picture of the people who inhabited the land at this time), some general inferences about these ancient Britons could be made only through excavation of the surrounding land and of nearby graves. Archaeologists have learned that during the approximately fifteen centuries of construction on Stonehenge, different groups of prehistoric people inhabited the area. In its early stages the people were more or less nomadic, preferring to live in small groups that could easily move to follow migrating game or seasonal cycles. By the time Stonehenge was completed, these ancient Britons were more firmly rooted, with established trade routes, woven textiles for clothes and blankets, and more advanced tools and weapons (different clans often were in competition with each other). The life expectancy of the prehistoric builders was very short—a person age thirty was considered quite old. Forty percent of the people died before the age of twenty, which corresponds to the age of the bone fragments found around Stonehenge. This means that Stonehenge, and the other ceremonial and burial sites, was most likely built by teenagers.

OTHER CIRCULAR STRUCTURES

Long before Stonehenge was envisioned, these ancient people honed their skills on hundreds of other ceremonial structures nearby. There are at least nine hundred stone circles dotting the landscape of England, Wales, Scotland, and Ireland. Sometimes the stones in these circles were set upright, as at Stonehenge, and sometimes smaller stones were piled atop one another in imitation of one large stone. Even more circles were made of wood, but few of these survived the elements. The very first circular construction, known as Robin Hood's Ball, is thought to date from 3900 B.C. It resides less than two and a half miles northwest of Stonehenge. Robin Hood's Ball consisted neither of stone nor wood but rather of two concentric circles of banks and ditches. Stonehenge is the only stone circle whose stones were brought from great distances and the only place where the stones were trimmed and lintels (the stones that lay across the top of the upright stones) were used.

Possibly an early model for Stonehenge was a monument, discovered through aerial photography between WWI and WWII, that archaeologists have named Woodhenge. Built around 2300 B.C., Woodhenge consisted of concentric rings of wooden posts and may have been used for the same types of activities as Stonehenge. Like many ancient monuments in Britain, it is visible today only through crop markings. Growing wheat will be darker over ground that has been previously dug up or has held posts or walls. It will be lighter over areas that are solid, undisturbed earth. These crop markings are responsible for pointing archaeologists to ancient sites that could not be detected at ground level.

Two miles to the east of Stonehenge lies a huge enclosure fifteen hundred feet in diameter called Durrington Walls. It once had banks thirty feet high that, like the ones built around Stone-

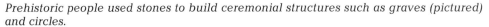

Prehistoric people used stones to build ceremonial structures such as graves (pictured) and circles.

henge, acted as protective barriers. It would have taken one hundred men around two and a half years to construct the earthen bank using antler picks and other animal bones fashioned into shovels. Inside the enclosure were two circular oak structures built around the same time as the first phase of Stonehenge. Archaeologists theorize that this area was a center of activity, but they still do not know what the area was designed for. Some speculate that this was where the people who built Stonehenge lived, but archaeologists have little conclusive evidence to support that claim.

Only twenty-five miles away in Avebury, a stone circle three times the size of Stonehenge was constructed during the late Neolithic period, six centuries before any stones were brought to Salisbury Plain. This "henge" is the largest in Europe, with a diameter of thirteen hundred feet (compared with Stonehenge's three hundred feet) and an outer bank that stood thirty feet high. The large outer circle was constructed of one hundred stones, within which were two smaller circles, one with twenty-nine stones, the other with twenty-seven. Each of these smaller circles contained yet another group of stones at its center. A road extending from the southeast part of the circle is lined with pairs of large stones in alternating (naturally occurring) rectangular and diamondlike angular shapes. Archaeologists have speculated that these may be male and female fertility symbols. Even though the Avebury circle is much larger than Stonehenge, its stones are local in origin and its design is not as intriguing or grand as its distant neighbor.

THE CURSUS

One of the few structures near Stonehenge that is not a circle or a burial mound is a nearly two-mile-long path running east to west just north of Stonehenge. First discovered by William Stukeley in 1723, this road (which goes nowhere) is roughly 330 feet wide, with two ditches and corresponding banks of dirt running parallel along both its sides. Stukeley believed it must have been a site for ancient road races and gave it the name cursus, the Latin word for racecourse. Like many of the ceremonial structures surrounding the monument, archaeologists still are not sure what actual purpose the Great Cursus, as it is known, served. The earthwork has been dated to around 3500 B.C., a few hundred years before the first building stage of Stonehenge.

This busy highway was preceded by an ancient road called the Great Cursus. Built around 3500 B.C., the cursus is older than Stonehenge itself.

The white chalk beneath the soil would have been visible in the ditches alongside the banks, making the cursus noticeable from quite far away. There is a huge burial site (called a long barrow) at the eastern end, leading to the theory that the cursus may have served as a processional path for funerals. There have been nearly fifty other cursuses discovered around Britain.

LONG BARROWS: COMMUNAL GRAVES
The hillsides surrounding Stonehenge are covered with hundreds of burial pits varying in size and shape. These prehistoric

earthworks were completed both before and during the early phases of Stonehenge's construction, and many contain chippings of the two types of stone used at Stonehenge. Communal burial was the choice of the earliest Stonehenge builders, and graves were dug deep into the earth and built of stone. These mass graves have been labeled long barrows by archaeologists. The largest held the remains of as many as forty people and assorted animal bones, and some vaults were so deep that a person could walk upright through them. Eighty percent of the long barrows that share Salisbury Plain with Stonehenge face in an easterly direction toward the point on the horizon where the sun rises, an alignment too frequent to be coincidental. Many ancient civilizations believed the sun had the power to restore life, and by orienting the graves toward the rising sun the builders were attempting to ensure their dead everlasting life.

DISCOVERIES IN ROUND BARROWS

Around 2500 B.C., as the Stone Age began to give way to the Bronze Age, communal graves went out of style and the new inhabitants of Salisbury Plain began burying their dead in individual graves called round barrows. At ground level these barrows look like nothing more than large mounds of earth or small hills. But these inconspicuous mounds that dot the countryside have revealed much to archaeologists. In the early 1800s archaeologist William Cunnington began digging up the graves in order to learn more about the people who built Stonehenge. He quickly discovered that the long barrows, although abundant in bones, held almost no buried goods. The round barrows, however, were often rich with objects that had been buried with their owners. No particular feature indicated a barrow's contents; as Cunnington noted, "the tiniest barrow might cover a rich grave, whilst under the finest might be only a bare skeleton." [4] Cunnington excavated more than six hundred graves during this time (two hundred of them very close to Stonehenge itself) under the direction of wealthy antiquarian Sir Richard Colt Hoare. Exhumed bones or cremated remains were always placed back in the earth and covered over again, and Cunnington left a brass token in each barrow with his or Colt Hoare's initials so archaeologists to come would know the grave had already been disturbed.

The greatest discoveries were made at Normanton Down, a huge concentration of burial barrows of different types a mile south of Stonehenge. Gold, amber, and bronze artifacts were uncovered in the round barrows at Normanton, evidently revealing the importance of the people buried there. One of the barrows, named the Bush Barrow, dates from around 2000 B.C., during the main phase of Stonehenge's construction in which the giant standing stones were raised. At Bush Barrow excavators uncovered a man's body that was laid out differently than all the others in the area. He was buried with his head pointing directly north, toward the stones. "This could be the man who built Stonehenge,"[5] says Dr. Paul Robinson, the curator of the Devizes Museum near Stonehenge, which leads the world in its collection of antiquities from the area. The man, clearly a chieftain, was found with two gold ornaments on his cloak, a hammered-gold hook on his belt, a mace with a smooth head of rare lime-

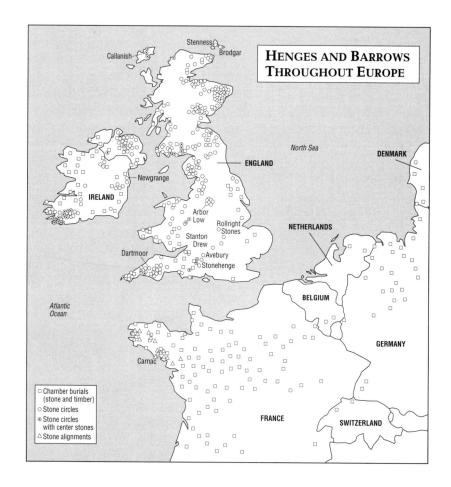

stone and a zigzag decoration on its wooden handle, and two daggers, one with a hilt inlaid with slivers of gold.

Of the hundreds of burial mounds around Stonehenge, none is within 164 yards of the monument itself. Apparently it was a great honor to be buried within sight of Stonehenge but forbidden to actually build a barrow on the site itself. Obviously the circle and its impressive stones held a great and perhaps spiritual significance for the people who labored to create the monument.

THE MUTE STONES SPEAK

In Elizabethan times people believed that the gigantic stones were not even real stones—that they were created in a giant kiln, like clay. This belief was widespread through the eighteenth century. Other theories proposed that the stones were "cast up from the earth . . . like arrows [shot] out of a volcano" or that they were "solid parts thrown out to the surface of the fluid globe, when its rotation was first impressed." [6] One hypothesis even contended that the rocks were debris from a space comet.

In fact, there are two types of stone at Stonehenge; though neither is indigenous to the Salisbury Plain, both can be found in other areas of the British Isles. The smaller of the two types is called bluestone, and the eighty-two bluestones selected for Stonehenge measure approximately eight feet tall and weigh around four tons each. Four different variations of bluestone have been found at Stonehenge. The one that was used most often is called dolerite, a greenish blue, coarse and grainy crystalline rock. Dolerite that is speckled with white or pinkish spots is called spotted dolerite to distinguish it from unspotted dolerite, which also appears at the site. Another variation of bluestone is called rhyolite, a type of volcanic lava with a hard flinty texture and a bluish gray color. The fourth variety is a dark olive green stone formed of volcanic ash with a texture softer than the others.

The other stones used at Stonehenge are called sarsens. They are the huge standing stones referred to in this description of the monument from 1562: "In a very extensive plain, at a great distance from the sea, in a soil which appeared to have nothing in common with the nature of stones or rocks are these masses of immense size almost every one of which, if you should weigh them, would be heavier than even your whole house." [7] A sarsen, two to three times harder than granite, is a natural form

NO WORDS CAN PROPERLY DESCRIBE

In his preeminent study, simply titled *Stonehenge*, Richard Atkinson poetically describes the beauty of the stones.

> Of the stones themselves no words of mine can properly describe the subtle varieties of texture and colour, or the uncountable effects of shifting light and shade. From a distance, they have a silvery grey colour in sunlight, which lightens to an almost metallic bluish-white against a background of storm clouds, an effect so notable it was recorded by [John] Constable [an English

The palette of color, shade, and texture in the stones ranges from polished and silvery to cracked and lichen-covered gray.

of sandstone and one of the hardest rocks on earth. The stones were formed when chalk deposits on the bottom of the seas were covered with sand. The sand hardened into blocks, and when the seabed rose the boulders broke the surface.

The Stonehenge sarsens forming the outer circle of the monument are huge, most weighing around 26 tons, some as much as 45 tons. They have an average width of 7 feet, a thickness of 3 to 4 feet, and are about 18 feet long. Some sarsens are buried as much as 5 feet into the soil so that all stand 13½ feet aboveground in a near perfect circle. Laid across the tops of the ring of sarsens are smaller sarsens called lintels. The lintels are painter who lived from 1776–1837] in his well-known water-colour. When the ground is covered in snow in midwinter, with a dull leaden sky threatening further falls, they seem nearly black; and at sunset in midsummer their surfaces glow, as if from within, with a soft warm pinkish-orange light. At a nearer view, each stone takes on its own individual pattern of colour and texture. Some are almost white, like coarse marble, with the sparkling grain of white lump sugar, and so hard that even 35 centuries of weathering has not dimmed the irregular patches of polishing executed so laboriously by the original builders. Others are a dull matt grey streaked and lined by close-set vertical cracks and fissures, like the grain of some vast stump of a petrified tree; and others again are soft, buff or even pink in colour, and deeply eroded into hollows and overhangs in which a man may crouch, the compact curves of his limbs and the rounded thrust of shoulder and hip matching the time-smoothed protuberances of the stone around him. On many of the surfaces, particularly on the lee side protected from the scouring force of wind and rain, there is a light growth of fluffy grey-green lichen, accented here and there by vivid patches of scaly yellow, which softens the contours of the stone, and half conceals, like a growth of fur, the scars left by those who have sought a little squalid immortality by the laborious incision of name or initials.

only about one-fourth the weight of the larger sarsens and measure on average 10½ feet long, 3½ feet wide, and 2½ feet thick. Today, most of the sarsens are covered with a filmy layer of grayish green lichen that hides the original brightness of the stones. At the time they were raised, the stones would have been a mosaic of blue, gray, green, and pearly pink.

Completely dwarfing the bluestones, the sarsens are the stones people think of when they think of Stonehenge. The bluestones, however, have the distinction of being the first stones brought to Stonehenge and were used in some capacity at every stage of the monument. They also came from much farther away than the sarsens; exactly how they got to Stonehenge is the subject of ongoing debate.

All four variations of bluestone come from only one source—within 20 miles of Mount Prescelly in southern Wales, 135 miles from Salisbury Plain. The specific mountaintop from which the outcrop of stones is believed to have been taken is called Carnmenyn. Stonehenge scholar Rodney Castleden calls this spectacularly rock-littered area "peculiar, almost setting itself apart as an alien and special place: it is instantly identifiable as a landmark from many kilometers away, a magnet for modern and prehistoric travelers alike, it would seem. From close up, it is strange, melodramatic, awe-inspiring—a place where gods might once have lived."[8] Archaeologists cannot say why these specific stones were chosen in spite of the extreme difficulty of transporting them at least 250 miles over land and water. One theory is that the stones were considered sacred and magical and that ownership brought great prestige. Another says they may have been a trade-gift from the local people to seal a friendly agreement over a trade route. Regardless of the reason why, figuring out how the rocks actually got to Salisbury Plain has kept archaeologists and engineers busy for centuries.

TRANSPORTING THE BLUESTONES

Researchers have advanced several theories of how both types of stones were transported from their natural environment to Salisbury Plain, although no hypothesis has been proven in the absence of surviving records. It is not even certain that the stones were moved and then used immediately; they could have been stockpiled for future use. Since no other stone circle in Britain was constructed with stones from farther away than five or six miles, transporting the stones to Stonehenge was an unprecedented feat. Most likely the bluestones were transported from Prescelly overland for sixteen miles to Milford Haven, then floated on rafts or canoed along the south coast of Wales to the Bristol Avon River, then dragged across the land for six miles to the River Wylye, and finally floated up the Hampshire Avon River to within two miles of Stonehenge. It is estimated that it would have taken sixteen men per ton of stone to move it overland, while only a dozen would have been needed to move the entire rock on water. The stones could have been floated between two canoes made of hollowed-out trees or on rafts made

PILGRIMAGE TO MOUNT PRESCELLY

In his book *Stonehenge of the Kings*, explorer Patrick Crampton relays his journey to Mount Prescelly, source of the Stonehenge bluestones, in southwest Wales. Crampton believed that to understand Stonehenge and the people who built it, he had to find out what was so special about this particular hillside, so very far from Salisbury Plain.

I was standing on Mount Prescelly, . . . turned to face the rushing wind and looked Westward. The valley of the River Nevern ran from me to make a shallow "V" eight miles off, partially framing a foreground of gray, silver and pale blue sea, which swept out to the horizon. Above, cumulus clouds sailed towards me in a cobalt sky, sailing from Ireland to Wales, just as the ships of the merchants with their gold, copper and valuable stone did when all roads, particularly that from Ireland, were drawn to the wealth of Stonehenge. How thankful the seamen must have been in bad weather to recognize the unmistakable shapes of the outcrops of bluestone on Mount Prescelly. The other mountains about stood smooth-domed. Only eastern Prescelly had these pinnacles of stone . . . upturned in their grain, so that rock-faces rose vertically in irregular, cubistic and trianguloid columns. Mount Prescelly clearly had particular significance to Neolithic and Bronze Age man. The widespread concept of gods living on mountains was a natural one. To the Greeks, Mount Olympus was the home of Zeus from antiquity into historic times, and this is how I regard Mount Prescelly. My senses were responsive to this long-awaited visit, and through Bronze Age eyes I could see the god . . . in the shape of a cloud and among the rocks. There was something akin to magic when I cracked a stone and a distinctive mottled surface appeared that was so familiar to me at distant Stonehenge. I found it satisfying to be looking at the evidence in my own hand of one of the greatest feats ever accomplished by a barbarian people anywhere in the world.

of wooden planks and animal skins. They would have been transported only in the summer, when the water was calm and the weather good. Though the water route added many miles to the trip, it would have saved up to 80 percent of the work required to carry the stones entirely over uneven terrain.

Researchers have also considered the possibility that these eighty-two bluestones were naturally deposited close to Salisbury Plain during an ice age 450,000 years ago. According to this

theory, an ice sheet picked the stones up and slowly moved them southeast along the Bristol Channel, then across dry land to Salisbury Plain. Thus the Stonehenge people would have gathered the stones from their own backyard rather than traveling 250 miles to get them. There are a few problems with this hypothesis, however. First, geologists have no evidence that glaciation occurred as far south in Britain as Salisbury Plain. Also, if an ice sheet did pick up the stones at Prescelly and carry them to Salisbury Plain, the area in between should have been littered with stones deposited along the way. There is, in fact, only one other bluestone between the two sites, and that was found near Stonehenge as part of a Neolithic barrow. Since there are no unused bluestones at the Stonehenge site, archaeologists argue that it is hard to believe that the exact number of bluestones needed for the monument were deposited there for the picking.

The other stones at Stonehenge—the sarsens—came from much closer to Stonehenge, but they are so much larger and heavier than the bluestones that archeologists wonder why they were used at all. The nearest source of sarsens was Marlborough Downs, twenty-four miles north of Salisbury Plain and east of the monument at Avebury. Other types of stone closer to the Stonehenge site certainly would have been more convenient to use, but most scholars believe the sarsens, like the bluestones, were chosen for a reason. Historians suggest that the giant stones were selected "on the basis of characteristics which would have had the maximum prestige, both for what they looked like, and in terms of the technical prowess needed to transport and work them."[9] It is possible that some of the smaller sarsens, perhaps the ones used for lintels, were taken from the Avebury monument itself, both because Avebury was a little closer to Salisbury Plain and because stones already dug out of the ground would have been easier to pick up. It is also possible that a few of the sarsens were already at the site itself, ready to be shaped for use in the monument.

TRANSPORTING THE SARSENS

The only feasible route from Marlborough Downs to Stonehenge is over land; experts doubt that the builders would have tried to maneuver the stones on the winding and shallow Avon River. To get from Marlborough Downs to the Stonehenge site the giant stones must have been transported twenty-four miles over a flat valley, across a stream, down a gentle slope, then down a moderately steep slope and across rolling plains. To explain how the stones were picked up and moved, historians look to the ancient Egyptians, who moved stones more than ten times heavier. If a stone was partially buried, deer antlers or primitive wooden or stone tools could have been used to pry the stone from its foundation. Then, long poles used as levers helped lift the stone off the ground and wooden supports held it up until the stone could be lowered onto a sledge of some sort that would bear the stone's weight.

Historically, it was believed the stones were probably transported on wooden rollers made from tree trunks. However, today's engineers think the stone's weight would have crushed the trees. British engineer Mark Whitby says, "I believe rollers were not used because the stones would tend to fall off. When you are shifting something heavy, you want to keep it going. I think the stones were dragged along a greased or iced surface such as one slippery plank on top of another, similar to a shipyard slipway." [10] In an experiment, Whitby pounded flat wooden rails into the ground, greased them with tallow (animal fat) and discovered that stones of similar size were pulled very easily over the tracks. Although Whitby's method worked well, there is no evidence that the builders of Stonehenge actually used this method, since any trace of wooden tracks would have long ago disappeared.

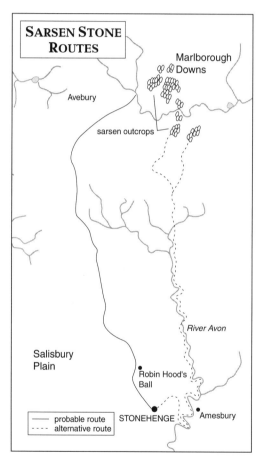

Ropes attached to a sledge of any design could have been made from animal hides or from the tough inner bark of certain trees indigenous to the area. Archaeologist Richard Atkinson deduced that it would have taken a team of more than a thousand men to haul one of the forty-five-ton sarsens, and that it would have taken at least ten years to get all the sarsens to Stonehenge. Some historians believe that oxen did the pulling rather than men, but others argue that prehistoric man had not yet begun harnessing animals in that capacity. Some also theorize that the movers might have shipped the stones in the winter, when the ground was covered with ice. It would have been easier to slide stones over icy ground, but much harder to control them. That the stones were moved through the Avebury circle at all awes modern-day stonemason Roger Hopkins: "Looking at this site, with all these stones in the way, it must have been a real chore to get these on a sled and get them out of this field." [11] Archaeologists admit they do not know how the stones got from one point to another, but one thing is certain—it must have been a very organized effort for a very important project.

A lot of work was done on the stones before they were transported to the Stonehenge site. Stonehenge is unique in that many of the bluestones and the huge sarsens were carefully molded and shaped to the builders' desired specifications. The technique of trimming and smoothing stone is called "dressing" the stone; as the sarsens were incredibly hard, it would have taken workers months just to dress a single stone. Most of the shaping would have been done before the stone was transported to make the stone that much lighter to move. Finishing, however, was done at Stonehenge before the stones were raised. The builders used axes or mauls made of sarsen rock to shape the stones, since no other material would have been strong enough to even dent the hard sarsens. It is possible that the builders used some abrasive substance like crushed flint to grind the surface a bit, but even constant hammering with mauls would remove only a fine dust. Scientists estimate that fifty stonemasons working ten-hour days, seven days a week, would have taken around two years and nine months to pound away two inches on all the stones. In order to break off large pieces, they would have had to use fire. First, they would scratch a line with a sharp rock where the break should occur. Then a flammable substance would be placed on the line and lit. When the fire burnt out, the ashes would be swept off and cold water would be poured over the still hot area. After that, the area would be weak enough to crack by pounding at it with stones. It is also possible that the builders used stone and wood wedges to split the sarsens. A crack would be made in the rock with the stone wedges, and then a piece of wood would be jammed into the crack. If water was poured on the wood it would expand enough to split the rock just a little bit more. A technique like this would have taken an incredibly long time, but eventually it would succeed in splitting the rock.

FINISHING TOUCHES

Once a stone fit the desired dimensions, it was dressed by pounding until the inner face of each upright sarsen was smooth. One pair of uprights supporting a lintel, called a trilithon, was smoothed on both inner and outer faces. Many of the smaller bluestones were even more carefully polished, and according to Atkinson, "It is one of the most curious features of Stonehenge that the art of dressing stones with such skill, and to shapes so aesthetically satisfying, should here have reached so high a pitch, and yet was not imitated, even in the crudest fashion, on any other British monument of later date." [12]

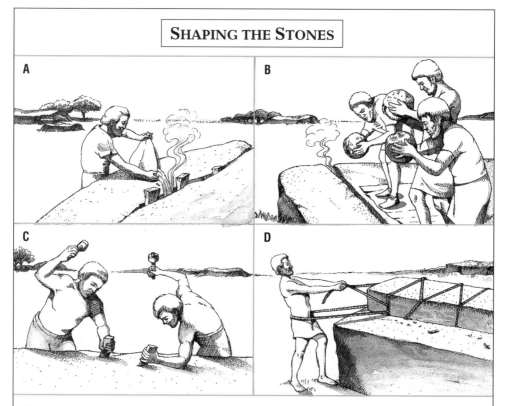

SHAPING THE STONES

A variety of techniques may have been used to shape and finish the stones: A) wedge and water; B) pounding cracks with stone mauls; C) chiseling the surface; D) smoothing the surface by rolling it back and forth over a stone covered with flint chips.

It is clear that the Stonehenge builders labored to make the monument as impressive as possible. In fact, as a final touch before raising the stones, the stonemasons shaped a slight convex curve into each of the upright blocks in the sarsen circle. This technique, which the Greeks called entasis, actually fools the eye into perceiving each column as perfectly straight.

The builders of Stonehenge had a greater understanding of building techniques and designs than historians originally believed. Twentieth-century archaeologists and builders have realized that during each stage of Stonehenge's existence, the builders had a specific plan in mind and laid it out with precision and care. That fact alone indicates something about these groups of people who have otherwise greatly eluded history.

Early Stages
of Construction

*It is hard not to envy those lonely discoverers [the ar-
chaeologists] left behind, with their shirt sleeves, their
broken nails, their pipes in the open air. Washed by the
rains of the plain, burnt by the sun, with minds intent
and happy, they sieve and sieve and then sieve again
that black and historic earth.*
                                    —*Times* of London, April 5, 1920

Stonehenge is more than the ruin of one stone monument; it is
actually the ruin of the last of five different structures built on
the same site by different peoples over fifteen centuries. Sometimes the builders reused or repositioned stones that the previous inhabitants had erected; sometimes they added entirely
new features. The early phases of Stonehenge set the stage for
the grander and more ambitious monuments of later generations. Fortunately, archaeologists, trained in excavating ancient
sites, have been able to piece together a picture of what these
phases entailed.

ARCHAEOLOGY AT STONEHENGE

It is the job of the archaeologist to find records of things that no
longer exist; in this case to discover exactly what parts of Stonehenge were built at what time, how they were built, and by
what sort of people. The answers are all hidden in the ground,
waiting to be reconstructed from shallow pits, pieces of burnt
carbon, scraps of bone, pottery, and stone shavings. If an object
is dropped on the surface of the ground, it will be buried in the
soil within a few years by rain washing the dirt over it, wind
blowing leaves and dust over it, and the activity of earthworms.
Archaeologists have determined that an object left on the
ground near Stonehenge one hundred years ago is now buried
six to eight inches below the ground.

Archaeological excavations have taken place at Stonehenge for nearly two hundred years, some doing more harm than good by destroying large sections of the site. In 1802 the first dig at Stonehenge itself was conducted by William Cunnington, who had already dug at many of the graves nearby. "I have this summer," he wrote, "dug in several places in the area and neighbourhood of Stonehenge (taking care not to go too near the stones) . . . and found charred wood, animal bones and pottery, of the latter there were several pieces similar to the rude urns found in the barrows." [13] He also uncovered a large barbed iron arrowhead, prehistoric British pottery, and Roman pottery, proving that Stonehenge had been around long before the Romans conquered the British Isles. Cunnington was warned by one of his patrons not to let his excitement get in the way of careful excavation of the land and the barrows. "You will excuse me I am sure," Thomas Leman writes in a letter,

> when I take the liberty of pointing out to you the necessity of *immediately pasting a small piece of paper on every piece of pottery*, or *coin* that you may hereafter find, describing with accuracy the very spot in which you find them. The people who succeed us, may probably know

HUMAN SACRIFICES AT STONEHENGE?

There are many accounts of animal and human sacrifice in ancient religious traditions and cultural practices. Men, women, and children were killed and presented to the gods as proof of their allegiance. By some accounts, the people who were killed were honored to be chosen since their deaths would ensure a good crop, a short rainy season, or fulfill some other public need. At Stonehenge one grave was found to contain a burial that may have been a sacrificial death. Sometime around 2130 B.C., during the second stage of the building of Stonehenge, a young man was killed with three arrows and then buried in the ditch where he fell. In the grave with him was found a stone wrist guard, implying that the man himself was an archer. The three arrows that killed him were found embedded in his ribs, obviously fired at close range from three different sides. Clearly he was murdered, but it is possible that his death was other than sacrificial. Perhaps he more about these things than we do . . . but we ought to afford *them* the information we can, with clearness.[14]

A hundred years later, in 1901, archaeologist William Gowland meticulously excavated an area around one of the sarsens and discovered more about the actual process of building the monument than anyone before him. He found the tools—all stone—that the builders had used and then tossed into the holes they had dug as resting places for the stones. This evidence of stone tools reinforced the belief that the builders were from the Neolithic period. Gowland also learned how the stones had been put into the holes by studying the soil deposits in the chalk. Unfortunately, not every excavating team was as protective of the site as those of Cunnington and Gowland. From 1919 to 1926 Colonel William Hawley, with little financial support from the government, dug up half of Stonehenge in such a haphazard way that he damaged the site for future excavators. Assisted by archaeologist Robert Newall, Hawley is credited with finding new series of stone holes and further investigating old ones. However, having discovered nothing more exciting than scraps of bones, chippings of stones, flint flakes, and shards of pottery, a frustrated Hawley believed that he knew no more

was a member of a warring clan; perhaps he offended the Stonehenge builders in some way. One theory holds that he was a builder himself, and that when the Stonehenge IIIa people took over the monument from the Stonehenge II people, he was one of their victims. A discovery at nearby Woodhenge, however, lends credence to the sacrifice scenario. When the foundation for Woodhenge was laid, around 2300 B.C., a three-and-a-half-year-old girl killed by an ax blow to her head was buried near the center of the structure in a ritual to bring good luck to the building project. Adding to speculation that there was sacrifice at Stonehenge was the discovery of three sets of adult and child graves spaced evenly around the east half of the bank. It is possible that when the west side of the bank is excavated more graves will be revealed. Did these people die natural deaths? Or were three sets of mothers and toddlers ritually sacrificed?

DEATH AT STONEHENGE

British author John Fowles is internationally known for his best-selling novels. He is also an authority on Stonehenge and describes a lifelong fascination with the subject, beginning with his first visit as a young boy. In his book *The Enigma of Stonehenge*, he contemplates the idea that archaeologists learn more about ancient people's deaths than about their lives.

> Death, alas, is a much better archaeologist's assistant than life, since it leaves so many more traces and clues behind it. A kind of variation of the pathetic fallacy—a mortician's fallacy—soon overcomes anyone who reads prehistoric archaeology: all seems death and disease, a brutish struggle in the nastiest of all possible worlds. Nothing is easier than to discover decayed teeth, poorly mended bone-fractures and signs of rickets in a Neolithic skeleton; to find a joy in dancing, a skill at fowling, a sense of humour, is impossible. We know not one single thing of the physical and emotional capacities, the thought-processes and sensitivities of these lost ancestors of ours. We may with an effort subtract all or most of our present culture and imagine what it would be like to live without it; but we can never begin to imagine the other side of the moon, the pleasures and rewards of the men and women who lived then. It is forever secret, undiggable, unpierceable.

about Stonehenge in 1926 than when he began digging. One of his more interesting discoveries was a bottle of wine that Cunnington had buried over 120 years earlier, with a note that read, "out of consideration for future excavators." Unfortunately for Hawley, the cork had rotted and most of the wine was gone.

ATKINSON'S EXCAVATION

Richard Atkinson, the most dedicated of Stonehenge archaeologists, began digging at the site in 1950 along with fellow archaeologists Stuart Piggott and J. F. S. Stone. Their job was to sort out the records Hawley left behind and develop a better understanding of the whole region. It is Atkinson who is credited with providing the first relatively clear idea of the building phases. Identifying four groups of builders, Atkinson nonetheless asserted that there were six distinct phases of construction, which he labeled Stonehenge I; Stonehenge II; Stonehenge IIIa, IIIb, and IIIc; and Stonehenge IV. The related phases of Stonehenge III were separated by decades while the more distinct phases were hundreds of years apart. Atkinson continued to reevaluate his findings as new research was completed, and his reports formed the basis for all subsequent excavation. He gives a lot of credit to archaeologist Sir Flinders Petrie (remembered primarily as an Egyptologist), who in 1880 created the most accurate map of Stonehenge ever published. Petrie also numbered all the stones in the monument, both those still standing and those long absent, and his numbering system is still used today. Atkinson did not agree, however, with his predecessor's notion of how much of Stonehenge should be excavated and how much should be left undisturbed. Petrie advocated digging up the whole area, while Atkinson thought it prudent to upset only what was absolutely necessary. A few years before his death in 1994, Atkinson said he did not think archaeologists should be allowed to dig at Stonehenge for at least seventy-five years, as each generation of archaeologists has thrown away or disturbed the exact finds that the next generation was looking for. "It would be a crime," he said, "for anyone to tackle Stonehenge again before we've learned to ask different questions." [15]

DATING STONEHENGE

Without the scientific means to accurately date objects found at Stonehenge, it would be nearly impossible to deduce the sequence of events that took place there. Prior to the mid–twentieth century, some scientists had tried to date Stonehenge by studying the position of the sun and stars over the stones. Under the assumption that the builders aligned the stones with the sunrise on the summer solstice, they determined the present position of the stones in relation to the sun and tried to affix a date by calculating backward, using the known change in the tilt of the earth's axis (one-seventeenth of a degree per century). Their calculations varied widely and were discounted quickly.

The guessing finally came to an end in 1949 with the invention of radiocarbon dating, a very reliable method of dating any material that was once alive, including human remains, animal bones and antlers, leather, and charcoal (the remains of plant material or wood).

All living tissue contains carbon atoms in two forms: a stable form, carbon 12, and a radioactive form, carbon 14, that is unstable and slowly disintegrates after death. The ratio of carbon 12 to carbon 14 in living tissue is 1 trillion to 1. After death, the amount of carbon 12 remains constant but one-half of the carbon 14 will disintegrate every 5,760 years. If scientists can determine how much of both forms of carbon atom are left in a piece of bone or charcoal, they can very accurately calculate the object's age. As one researcher illustrates:

> Suppose that when the plant was alive it had 100 trillion atoms of carbon 12. It would therefore have had 100 atoms of carbon 14. If a scientist, in examining the charcoal from an ancient fire, found only 50 atoms of carbon 14 for the 100 trillion atoms of carbon 12, he would know that the charcoal was 5,760 years old. Similarly, if he found only 25 carbon 14 atoms, the charcoal would be twice that old—or 11,520.[16]

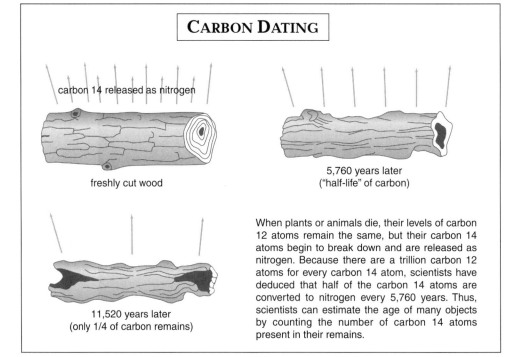

CARBON DATING

carbon 14 released as nitrogen

freshly cut wood

5,760 years later
("half-life" of carbon)

11,520 years later
(only 1/4 of carbon remains)

When plants or animals die, their levels of carbon 12 atoms remain the same, but their carbon 14 atoms begin to break down and are released as nitrogen. Because there are a trillion carbon 12 atoms for every carbon 14 atom, scientists have deduced that half of the carbon 14 atoms are converted to nitrogen every 5,760 years. Thus, scientists can estimate the age of many objects by counting the number of carbon 14 atoms present in their remains.

BEFORE RADIOCARBON DATING

Before the invention of radiocarbon dating in 1949, other methods of placing an object in historical context were necessary. The most widely practiced method, known as "sequence dating," requires a so-called baseline sample; that is, an authentic object with a clearly established date, such as a coin stamped with the face of a historical figure, or a tombstone with burial dates. Another accepted baseline sample might be a tomb sealed since a certain known date and then opened; archaeologists can confidently conclude that the artifacts found inside were created before the tomb was sealed, thereby placing them within a more or less specific time period. These objects would then become part of the time line of that particular region. It is possible, then, to place a certain object close in time to another object by noting its similar and dissimilar characteristics. For instance, as famed archaeologist and Egyptologist Sir Flinders Petrie discovered, the sizes of the handles on clay jars from a particular region gradually got smaller over time. A researcher trying to date a newly discovered jar could compare its handles with the handles of similar jars to determine where to place it on the already established time line of jars from that area. This comparison method of dating is not very precise and can only provide the scholar with limited information, but before radiocarbon dating it was the most widely practiced way to assign an object or even a whole site to a sequence in time.

By testing once-living materials unearthed from different sections and layers of Stonehenge, it was finally possible to figure out when the stones adjacent to those materials were raised, lowered, or otherwise moved and by what kinds of societies. Scientists learned that Stonehenge had been built over a period of twelve hundred years—roughly fifty-five generations of people could have worked on it.

STONEHENGE I (CA. 3100–2500 B.C.)

Using radiocarbon dating on one of the deer antlers that was found at the site, scientists estimate that the first phase of

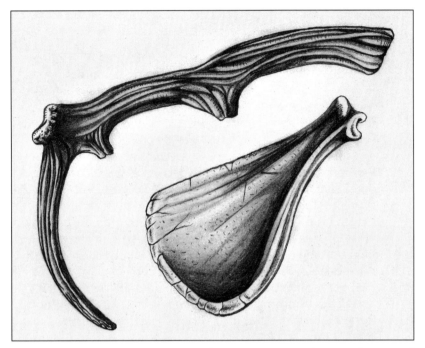

During the early phases of Stonehenge's construction, workers used picks made from deer antlers (left) and shovels fashioned from oxen shoulder blades.

Stonehenge's construction took place around 3100 B.C.. This stage in Atkinson's time line is known as Stonehenge I. Neolithic workers set out to create a nearly perfect circle (its diameter close to 320 feet) out of soil and chalk using only stone tools and animal bones. They most likely pounded a wooden stake into the ground at the point that was to be the center of the circle, attached a long rope to it (approximately 160 feet long), and marked the circular path of the rope's unattached end. Workers, using pickaxes made from red deer antler and shovels made from the shoulder blades of oxen, then dug deep pits into the chalky earth all the way around the circle. Most of the pits were then connected, forming a fairly continuous ditch running the circumference of the circle and an earthen embankment of the displaced soil. They left a wide opening on the northeast side for the main entrance into the circle, and a small gap on the southeast side may have been left there to form a smaller, alternate entrance.

The ditch varied in depth from 4½ to 7 feet and was about 20 feet wide. Since the chalk below the surface is bright white, the ditch would have been in stark contrast to the black soil. Nevertheless, Atkinson believes that the ditch itself may not have been very important to the builders; in fact, he suggests that the inner bank formed from the soil dug from the ditch was meant to be the significant feature. Atkinson believes this earthen wall would have stood 6 feet high and 20 feet wide (as wide as the ditch outside it). Today, the bank only stands a few inches above the ground, but at the time, it must have served as formidable protection for whatever activities took place within the circle. There is some evidence that there was another, smaller bank on the outer side of the ditch. Atkinson believes this bank would have been about 8 feet wide and 2½ feet tall. Rain and wind would have worn down the banks very quickly, and it is likely that visitors to Stonehenge two thousand years ago would not have seen them much more clearly than modern-day visitors do.

THE CAUSEWAY

The northeast opening of the embankment, called the causeway, was about thirty-five feet wide. Aligned with the rising sun on the summer solstice, historians believe this was supposed to be the ceremonial entrance into the center of the circle. The smaller entrance to the southeast would have been the common entrance. Researchers currently believe that during the Stonehenge I period there were two stones (long gone, but archaeologists assume they were indigenous to the area) that guarded either side of the causeway. Also situated around the causeway are rows of random wooden postholes, which may have been dug before the ditch. At one time it was assumed they supported posts used for some sort of wooden gateway to the circle, but there are too many holes in a seemingly haphazard pattern to make that scenario likely. Some have speculated that they held wooden stakes whose purpose was to chart the moonrise to its northernmost point. But there are so few traces of these posts left on the ground that it is impossible to accurately discern their purpose. There are also four postholes sixty-five feet past the causeway entrance that are more likely to have served as footings for a gate than the others. Even though there is limited evidence of postholes in the center of the circle, most archaeologists believe that a hut or roundhouse building was constructed there out of wood during this phase and dismantled when the stones were brought in during later phases of Stonehenge.

THE HEEL STONE

Only one stone still stands that can definitively be said to have been part of Stonehenge I, and that is the Heel Stone. It stands about 85 feet outside the causeway entrance along a northeasterly path to the circle. This huge sarsen boulder is untrimmed, more than 8 feet wide, and stands 16 feet tall buried 4 feet into the ground. In 1979 another stone hole was found 12 feet northwest of the Heel Stone. Researchers speculate that the two were meant to be a pair, mimicking the two set up closer to the causeway entrance. On the morning of the summer solstice, when the sun is at its closest point to the earth, the sun rises between the Heel Stone and its now missing partner.

Like all the "named" stones at Stonehenge, the Heel Stone's title has no certain link with the stone's actual or supposed purpose. Since the stone's use was almost certainly connected with the midsummer sunrise, the name was once believed to be derived from the Greek word *helios*, meaning sun. When researching the first time the Heel Stone was found in print, however, archaeologist Richard Atkinson traced it back to an unpublished manuscript by John Aubrey that challenges the helios association. In 1660, Aubrey related a legend he had heard about the devil throwing one of the stones at a town friar because the friar was unable to tell him how many stones were in

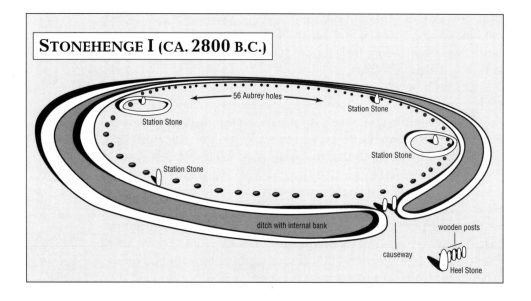

STONEHENGE I (CA. 2800 B.C.)

56 Aubrey holes

Station Stone

Station Stone

Station Stone

Station Stone

ditch with internal bank

wooden posts

causeway

Heel Stone

the circle. The stone supposedly hit the friar on the heel and the stone became dented in the shape of a heel, giving birth to the name Heel Stone. As it turns out, Aubrey was referring to a stone on the other side of Stonehenge, and for some reason history reassigned the legend to the stone now standing outside the entrance to the monument.

THE AUBREY HOLES

One of the most unusual features of Stonehenge I is the 56 shallow pits that lie in a circle inside the perimeter of the earthen bank. These pits were first discovered in 1666 by John Aubrey, who was then surveying the site for King Charles II. Aubrey found 5 shallow cavities in the ground just inside the bank, jotted that observation down in his notes, and moved on. In 1920, Robert Newall convinced William Hawley to follow Aubrey's lead, and they discovered that the pits continued all the way around the circle and numbered 56. Now known as the Aubrey holes in honor of their discoverer, the pits are set approximately 16 feet apart around a circle with a diameter of 288 feet. They are roughly 2 to 4 feet deep and 2½ to 5 feet wide and have steep sides and flat bottoms. The same tools and animal bones would have been used to dig them as were used to create the ditch. The Aubrey holes never held stones, nor is it likely they held wooden posts, and they were apparently refilled soon after they were dug. But the holes were not empty. Thirty-four of the 56 holes have been excavated, and nearly all of them contained human cremated remains. This leads archaeologists to believe that the Aubrey holes were ritual burial pits, although they are still unsure if the inhabitants died natural or sacrificial deaths.

A LONG GAP

In 1978 archaeologist John Evans reopened an area excavated by Atkinson and dug all the way down to the prebuilding phase. By examining the remains of different types of prehistoric snail shells, he was able to determine that after the initial building of Stonehenge I, the site must have been deserted for a few hundred years. Since the different species of snail thrive in different kinds of terrains, their presence at different times would indicate what type of landscape prevailed in that region. The snail shells indicated that after Stonehenge I, vegetation and woodlands were allowed to grow over the site. Why the builders abandoned their creation is unclear; perhaps they moved on to work on other structures in the area, such as Durrington Walls and Woodhenge. Actually, during this time Stonehenge may have been more neglected than totally abandoned; cremated burials were still being performed there, filling the Aubrey holes and wide areas of the ditch and bank.

THE STATION STONES

There is one element of Stonehenge that was either constructed right before the long period of abandonment or right after it—the positioning of the four Station Stones. These relatively small sarsens were erected in a perfect rectangle inside the bank, obliterating the Aubrey holes beneath them. Two of these stones are still in place today, but their purpose continues to puzzle archaeologists. One theory is that the Station Stones are aligned to mark the important change of seasons—that the position of the sun on a particular day as it hits the individual stones indicates the midsummer sunrise or the midwinter setting of the moon, and that the diagonal of the rectangle points to the May Day sunset. It is clear that the stones were erected after the Aubrey holes were dug but before any of the center stones were brought to the site. This would place their appearance either at the end of Stonehenge I or at the beginning of Stonehenge II. Contemporary surveyors believe that the Station Stones were most likely set up after Stonehenge I to help the builders calculate the proportions of the stone circle they were soon to build. This hypothesis seems credible because an imaginary diagonal line drawn between the stones marks the center of the future stone circles, whereas they are a bit farther to the north of the center of Stonehenge I. One of the Station Stones was carefully trimmed, a practice that did not characterize sarsens until Stonehenge III. This leads archaeologists to believe that it was probably a replacement of an untrimmed stone that had either broken or been removed.

STONEHENGE II (CA. 2500–2100 B.C.)

Construction of Stonehenge II roughly coincided with the building of the pyramids in Egypt and the great temples of ancient Babylon. This phase of Stonehenge's construction may have been instigated by a different people than had previously inhabited the area. The Beaker Folk, named for the sophisticated pottery they left behind, showed marked cultural differences from their predecessors. Their society was hierarchical, headed by chiefs and spurred on by trade with others. Colorful woven textiles replaced animal hides as clothing, and warriors wore bronze armor. Round barrow graves with single occupants replaced the communal long barrows.

THE AVENUE

The Beaker Folk made a number of changes to the Stonehenge I design. They widened the causeway by filling in portions of the ditch. The center of the newly expanded entrance was aligned more exactly on the axis of the midsummer sunrise, and the two stones that had stood at either side of the entrance were moved to the new width. The Beakers then constructed a road leading up to the causeway. This road, now known as the Avenue, was

The Station Stones, two of which are still visible, formed a rectangle just inside the circular bank. These stones may have served as a guide for the inner ring of stones.

flanked by two parallel banks about forty feet apart running northeast out of the site. Thirty-five-foot-wide ditches ran along the outside of the banks. The Avenue extends for more than a mile, veering to the east and then turning in a southeasterly direction to the bank of the River Avon. As it proceeds, the Avenue gradually widens until it eventually measures roughly seventy-five feet across.

Today no physical signs indicate that the Avenue extended completely to the edge of the river, but it seems logical that that was the case. That would help explain why the Avenue takes a slightly roundabout route to get from Stonehenge to the riverbank, since the stone movers would have wanted to avoid traversing steeper areas. There are also signs that stones were set up along either side of the Avenue, but none exist today. It would take further excavation to verify their existence and figure out what type of stones they were and when they were removed. Some historians believe that the Avenue was only five hundred yards long during the construction of Stonehenge II, and that a thousand years would pass before the Avenue was extended to the riverbank during Stonehenge IV.

THE BLUESTONE CIRCLES

Early in the building of Stonehenge II, the first bluestones were brought to the site. At this time the Beakers set up a mound of earth around the Heel Stone, possibly to protect it while they dragged the four-ton bluestones past. Since there is no evidence of an adjacent mound, archaeologists surmise that the Heel Stone's partner was already missing, or that the new builders removed it for some reason, perhaps with the intention of setting it back up when they were done transporting the bluestones. Similar protective banks surrounded two of the Station Stones as well. Again, it is still not clear whether the Beaker people originally set up the Station Stones or merely used them to their advantage when calculating the center of their bluestone circles.

The eight-feet-high bluestones were then carefully dressed, many until they were perfectly smooth on both sides and top. To researchers, this indicates that even at this early phase of construction, the project was considered an important and unique undertaking. After the stones were dressed, the builders began setting them up in two concentric rings (with an outer and inner

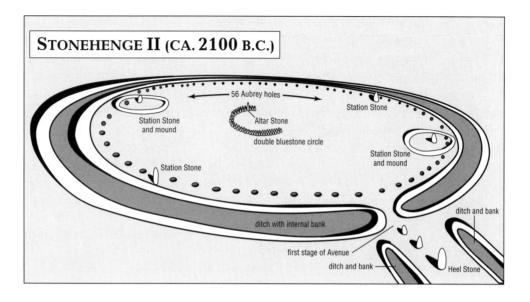

STONEHENGE **II** (CA. 2100 B.C.)

56 Aubrey holes

Station Stone

Station Stone
and mound

Altar Stone

double bluestone circle

Station Stone
and mound

Station Stone

ditch and bank

ditch with internal bank

first stage of Avenue

ditch and bank

Heel Stone

diameter of eighty-six and seventy-four feet, respectively) a bit off from the center of Stonehenge I. For some reason, the Beakers did not complete the circles. According to archaeologists the Beaker Folk left or were driven away from Salisbury Plain by 2000 B.C. This may be why the bluestone circles were never completed, or perhaps the builders had already decided in favor of building an even more impressive monument and voluntarily stopped work on the current layout. It is even feasible that the Beakers had run out of bluestones of sufficient size.

By 2100 B.C. the bluestones that had already been set upright were removed (either by the Beakers or by the group who took their place), and the holes were filled in. The holes that the bluestones were removed from are now referred to as Q and R holes and little trace of their existence remains on the surface. The pattern of the holes, as determined by archaeologists, would indicate that eighty-two stones were originally figured into the design, and it is possible that other bluestones were designated as lintels and were either laid or designated to be laid on top before the plan was abandoned. At least one-quarter of each circle was never completed. It also appears that extra stones were placed in rows extending out from the circles toward the entrance to the Stonehenge I banks and ditch, giving the impression of a threshold through which people would pass to enter the inner circles.

THE ALTAR STONE

Directly across from the "threshold" entrance into the inner bluestone circles stood one of the most unusual stones erected at Stonehenge during any phase. Long toppled over its own hole, the Altar Stone is 16 feet long, 3½ feet wide, and 1¾ feet deep. The stone is neither a bluestone nor a sarsen but rather a type of sandstone from the Cosheston Beds on the shores of Milford Haven. This area is in Wales, south of Prescelly, and the stone might have been picked up by the builders as they passed by the region with their cargo of bluestones. The Altar Stone is pale green embedded with tiny fragments of mica and garnet and, when upright, would have towered high over the bluestone circles. This stone, like the bluestones, was removed and reused in following phases of Stonehenge's construction.

The Altar Stone got its name because of its current appearance, lying flat like an altar in the center of the ring of sarsens brought during the building of Stonehenge III. Since it is now known that at one time the Altar Stone actually stood upright as the focal point of the monument, it clearly had some special meaning to the Stonehenge people, although not as an altar. Historians believe it may have been considered an idol of some sort—a dwelling place for or a symbol of a god or goddess. What is evident, however, is that the stone's importance, whatever that was, carried over into Stonehenge III as well.

Later Stages of Construction

3

Why the Beakers disappeared from Salisbury Plain remains a mystery; excavations show that their pottery is no longer found there after about 2100 B.C. The next people to work on Stonehenge were from the Wessex culture. Some archaeologists believe that these people may have been the descendants of the very first group to work on Stonehenge nearly a thousand years before. A larger and more organized society, the Wessex people worked on the third stage of Stonehenge's construction. Atkinson broke this stage down into three distinct phases: Stonehenge IIIa, IIIb, and IIIc, because each of these phases witnessed significant changes in the monument's appearance. The three phases of Stonehenge III were most likely constructed by the descendants of the Wessex culture over many centuries, and it was during this time that the new builders altered the configuration of the existing bluestones and brought in the giant standing stones that characterize Stonehenge today.

STONEHENGE IIIA (CA. 2100–2000 B.C.)

The precision, innovation, and workmanship of the Stonehenge III stonemasons had no match in prehistoric Europe. The layout of the stones for Stonehenge III was much more complex than anything previously attempted at the site, and much forethought must have gone into its planning. As soon as the bluestone circles from Stonehenge II were dismantled and the holes filled, it was possible for the new builders to map out their design. The huge sarsen stones were brought to the site from Marlborough Downs, twenty-four miles away. While prehistoric engineers were designing the structure, stonemasons would have been measuring the stones and painstakingly smoothing them. The work required to fashion the sarsens into closely matching rectangular shapes had probably already been done before they were transported. Any smoothing and dressing of the stones,

CARVINGS

One day, while archaeologist Richard Atkinson was studying some old graffiti on the face of a particular stone, he noticed what appeared to be prehistoric carvings of a dagger and four ax heads. Over the next few weeks more carvings of axes were found on other stones and the excitement mounted. One carving looks like a rectangular shield but is now believed to be a representation of a goddess figure, a common sight in prehistoric Europe. Neolithic scholar Rodney Castleden has calculated a relationship among all the carvings in his book *The Making of Stonehenge.*

> In order to understand [the carvings] fully, we need to look at Stonehenge in plan. When their positions are plotted on a plan an interesting pattern emerges. The goddess drawing lies to the west of the monument's center, the dagger and axes on stone 53 to the south: in other words, they mark cardinal compass points. The carvings on the stones in the sarsen circle fall into the

however, was completed at Stonehenge before the stones were erected and is confirmed by the large amounts of sarsen dust discovered deep in the earth. There was quite a bit of dressing involved; all of the sarsens taper in toward the top with approximately five inches chiseled off both sides, and one full face of each stone (the side that would eventually face the inside of the circle) was smoothed. The lintels were also slightly curved so when set in place they formed a smooth round circle.

It is unclear what the Stonehenge III builders did with the bluestones from the circles that had been dismantled at the end of Stonehenge II. They were either stored somewhere nearby or, as some historians believe, used to build some other neighboring structure. There is no evidence, however, that they were used in any way during this time.

DESIGNING THE SARSEN CIRCLE AND HORSESHOE TRILITHON

The first thing the builders needed to do was to figure out the exact center for the initial part of construction—a new, wide circle of sarsens that would support a ring of stones running across same pattern. Axes carved on the outer faces of stones 3, 4, and 5 mark the east. The small goddess symbol, which would have been very hard to see against the sky, cut into the underside of circle lintel stone 120, was originally placed in the gap between the two uprights on the west side of the circle. Now that the lintel lies on its back on the ground, the goddess symbol is visible as a rectangular, 1 cm deep rebate cut right across the width of the stone. One side is dead straight, the other is disturbed by a natural pit which made the carvers place the head to one side, but the projection representing the head is plainly recognizable. Here, once more, we come face to face with the goddess whose temple this was. Three cardinal compass directions were signed by the carvings — east, south and west — though not the north, and that was presumably because neither the sun nor the moon ever appears in the northern sky.

the top. This could have been done by using the four Station Stones as markers to map out the center as the Beakers most likely had done a few centuries before. If they stretched a length of string between each diagonal pair of Station Stones, the point where the strings intersected would give them an approximate center. They also may have tried to use the Aubrey holes or the bank itself as guides, although these would have been more inexact and time-consuming methods.

Once the center was fixed, the placement of each of the thirty sarsens around the circumference of the circle would have to be marked. The diameter of the circle was a little under 100 feet. In order to space the sarsens evenly around the circle, wooden stakes would have been pounded into the ground at the point coinciding with the center of each stone, at intervals of exactly 10½ feet. Each stone was around 3½ feet thick and 7 feet wide; thus, a space of 3½ feet was left between each stone. An extra gap of 1 foot was left between the two sarsens closest to the northeast entrance of the Avenue to emphasize the pathway into the circle.

With the layout of the sarsen circle marked on the ground, the builders turned to planning and erecting the five trilithons in

The trilithon consists of a lintel placed atop two upright sarsens. Together, the five trilithons form a horseshoe in the center of Stonehenge.

the center of the circle. The word *trilithon* literally means "three stones." At Stonehenge, each set of three stones comprises two upright sarsens with a smaller sarsen (a lintel) laid across their tops. The builders designed the trilithons so that they would form a horseshoe shape, with the open end aligned with the northeast entrance of the henge. Each side of the horseshoe consists of two trilithons, with a fifth trilithon in the center of the horseshoe's curve. The trilithons on each side gradually increase in height; the one at the head of the horseshoe is the tallest of all and is referred to as the Great Trilithon. The first pair on each side is 20 feet tall, the second pair is 21½ feet tall, and the Great Trilithon looms 24 feet above the ground. It is presumed that the Great Trilithon had some special purpose because its two uprights are the only stones at Stonehenge whose interior and exterior faces are both smoothed and polished. Atkinson suggests that this indicates "that one of the principal ritual stations in the monument may have been *behind* this trilithon, from which these surfaces would have been visible." [17] The fact that only the inner faces of the sarsens in the circle are smooth is taken to mean that what took place inside the circle was more important, or sacred, than what happened outside of it.

Once the trilithons were in place, the builders could work on the sarsen circle again. They had determined that despite the varied length of the stones each sarsen would be 13½ feet above the ground, i.e., the tops would all be level. When the smaller sarsens (the lintels) were placed around the ring on top of the uprights, the height rose to about 16 feet. Each carefully dressed lintel in the continuous circle is about 10½ feet long, 3½ feet wide, and 2¾ feet thick. Of the 30 sarsens in the original circle,

17 remain in position today, 8 have fallen, and the other 5 have been removed from the site over the centuries.

ERECTING THE STONES

Raising two fallen sarsen uprights in 1958 required the lifting capacity of the strongest crane in England. It has mystified people for centuries how prehistoric people, using only tools of wood, stone, and animal bones, were able to erect the massive stones (each weighing between twenty and forty-five tons) and to secure them so well in the ground that they would stand for thousands of years. Only in recent years have archaeological excavations been able to piece together the steps the builders took and to recognize the knowledge of physics and engineering required to accomplish the task.

In order to have 13½ feet of stone showing above ground, the depth that each stone would have to be buried depended on the

A 1958 photo of Stonehenge shows a crane lifting an eighteen-ton lintel. The lintel, which had fallen on its side, was placed upright in its correct position.

original length of the individual stone. The stones in the sarsen circle were sunk between 3 and 5 feet into the ground, while one of the uprights of the Great Trilithon was sunk 8 feet below the ground. Once the necessary depth was established, the hole would be dug accordingly, leaving up to a foot of extra room on each side. Three sides of the hole were vertical, but the side facing out of the circle sloped at a 45-degree angle, forming a ramp for the stone to slide down into the hole. Opposite the ramp side, the builders placed rows of wooden stakes to reinforce the side of the hole so that when the stone slid in and hit that side it would not drag soil and chalk underneath it.

The stone would then have been dragged toward the hole, most likely on logs or on a slight ramp of wooden planks, until the base of the stone projected over the sloped edge of the hole. The builders would then shift the stone's center of gravity until it was unbalanced and slid forward into the hole. This could have been achieved by maneuvering the material underneath the stone until it angled forward or by dragging heavy slabs of rock along the top of the stone until it passed the center and tipped the stone into the hole.

RAISING THE STONES UPRIGHT

With the stone sticking out of the hole at nearly a 45-degree angle, the next job was to pull it upright. Modern-day reenactments (and shadows of postholes in the ground) have proven that this was probably achieved by setting pieces of timber into an A-frame, which would act like a lever. Large groups of workers (numbering somewhere between 140 and 200) would pull long ropes (the same kind that they used to transport the stones) attached to the apex (the top) of the wooden structure. A shorter length of rope would be tied to the crossbar of the structure and then secured around the top of the stone. Pulling at acute angles to the structure, the workers would exert a force that would tip the A-frame, which in turn would exert a greater force on the shorter rope, pulling the stone upright. Erecting a leverage system like this would have greatly lessened the amount of energy it would have taken to raise the stones. It is possible, though unlikely, that no labor-saving device was used at all, just men with ropes. They could have attached ropes around the top of a leaning stone, and one team of men would have pulled on the rope while another group pushed on the stone from the other side.

The sheer weight of these large sarsens makes that scenario un-likely, although it is possible that this simplistic method was used to raise and straighten the smaller bluestones.

Once the stone was pulled into an approximately vertical po-sition, it would most likely still need to be adjusted. The base of each stone was somewhat pointed so that it would be fairly easy to rock the stone back and forth if it had to be lowered another inch or shifted a few degrees. When the stone was finally in per-fect position, the extra space left in the hole around the base and sides of the stone was packed tightly with rocks and boulders. Once the job was done, the builders often discarded used antler picks or other digging tools into the holes, and it is from radiocar-bon dating these objects that archaeologists have been able to date this period of Stonehenge's construction so accurately.

VARYING PERCEPTIONS OF STONEHENGE

In a letter written in 1743, William Stukeley described his excitement at wandering through Stonehenge:

> When you enter the building, whether on foot or horseback, and cast your eyes around the yawning ruins, you are struck into an ecstatic reverie, which none can describe, and they only can be sensible of it, that feel it. Other buildings fall by piece-meal: but here a single stone is a ruin, and lies like the haughty carcass of Goliath. . . . When we advance further, the dark part of the pon-derous imposts over our heads, the chasm of sky between the jambs of the cell, the odd construction of the whole, and the greatness of every part surprises.

A different reaction is expressed by Aubrey Burl in his 1987 book, *The Stonehenge People*. Burl found Stonehenge to be

> a dark place, oppressive as though Death were lurking in its shad-ows. The sarsens are thick, crowding against each other, forced deep into the ground by the lintels heavily pressing down upon them. It is a jostle of stone, monumental but overbearing, and the gaps between the pillars are no more than slits of light through the dark stonework of the circle. Inside the barrier of the sarsens the trilithons climb tightly together, shadowing the sky, grim, somber, elegiac as though mourning the twilight of mortality.

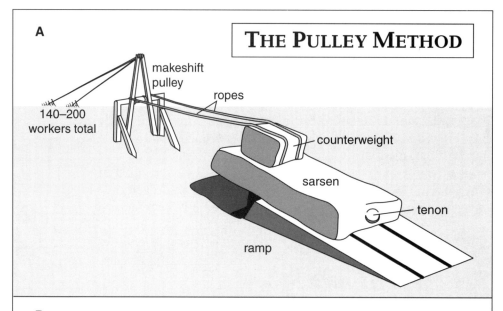

A

THE PULLEY METHOD

makeshift pulley

ropes

140–200 workers total

counterweight

sarsen

tenon

ramp

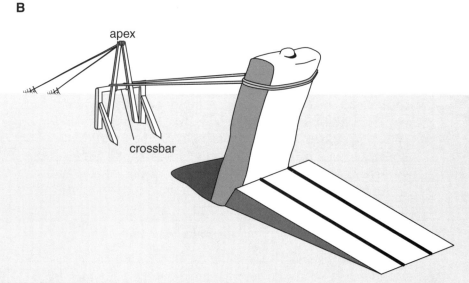

B

apex

crossbar

Researchers believe the builders of Stonehenge may have used a pulley system to lower the sarsens into their holes and straighten them once they were in place. The above diagram shows (A) how ropes and a counterweight could have been secured to the sarsens, allowing 140 to 200 workers to lower it into the hole using the A-frame pulley. After the sarsen was lowered (B) workers would then attach ropes from the top of the stone to the pulley's crossbar and straighten the sarsen from its 45° tilt.

THE LINTELS

The idea of a complete circle of stones resting atop the standing sarsens was unique to Stonehenge. There is no doubt that the builders took extra care with the appearance of the lintels since the workmanship on them is careful and precise. Each lintel was carefully dressed so that the inner and outer faces were smooth and curved gracefully around the circle, and the tops were ground until they were almost perfectly level. After all this preparation, the lintels were not simply laid on top of the uprights. Rather, they were firmly secured by mortise-and-tenon joints and by toggle joints (also known as tongue-and-groove joints). On the top face of each sarsen upright the builders carved out a pair of round knoblike projections (tenons) about 6 inches across and 3 inches high. On the underside of the lintels were corresponding hollow pits (mortises) that fit snugly over the projections, securing the lintels in place. The toggle joints were added to join the lintels to one another. A vertical groove was carved into one side of each lintel and then a projection was formed on the adjacent lintel to slide into the groove. Despite these strong stabilizing measures, of the original 30 lintels, 2 are in pieces on the ground, 6 remain in place, and 22 are missing.

RAISING THE LINTELS

Before the lintels could be raised and set atop the sarsen uprights, the uprights were allowed to settle into their new holes. Some engineers suggest that the sarsens may have been left to rest for as long as a year so that the builders would be sure that the added weight of the lintels would not cause the uprights to sink or shift out of balance. The builders could have used one of several methods to put up the lintels. There is no way the lintels could have been carried or lifted up since each weighed about four tons. Therefore, they either had to be pulled up a wooden or earthen ramp, or raised inch by inch by jamming logs underneath, lifting one side at a time. Unfortunately, there is no hard archaeological evidence of the actual process. In 1993, when modern-day men tried to raise a lintel using prehistoric methods, they found that dragging the lintel up a wooden ramp (with the help of the A-frames again) was a very efficient method. However, while this method certainly achieved its goal, there are no timber postholes that would prove the existence of a wooden scaffold or ramp being moved systematically around the circle.

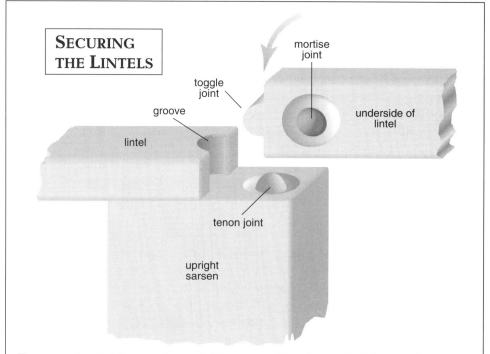

SECURING THE LINTELS

mortise joint

toggle joint

groove

underside of lintel

lintel

tenon joint

upright sarsen

To secure the lintels atop the upright sarsens, Stonehenge builders used mortise, tenon, and toggle joints. Two tenons, or knoblike projections, were carved on the top of the upright stone. Corresponding with the tenons were mortises, or hollow pits, bored into the underside of the lintels. Once the lintel was lifted on top of the upright, the mortise would slip securely over the tenon, securing it in place. Toggle, or tongue-and-groove, joints were also used to secure each lintel to its neighboring stone, much in the manner pieces of a jigsaw puzzle are connected.

Ramps made of earth and rock had been used in Egypt for centuries to raise stones, and the Stonehenge people would certainly be aware of this method since they had already raised timber buildings using ramps. Again, however, there is no evidence that any of the surrounding land was used to form what would have been huge ramps, nor is it likely that the builders would have been able to easily disassemble and reassemble the mounds at the next section of the circle.

The possibility that the lintels were raised by jacking up one side then the other while shoving logs or rectangular-shaped wooden timbers underneath has been given serious thought. Once one layer was complete, a lever would be used to jack up one end of the lintel again, and then another row of timbers would be laid underneath it facing the opposite direction. The main criticisms of this idea are that it would take an extremely long time to raise a stone this way, and an extremely large amount of timber (about a mile's worth). It is certainly possible that the Stonehenge builders were willing to put the time and effort into cutting down the trees and shaping them into rectangular blocks at least twenty feet long because they would be able to reuse the same wood for the entire project. Many engineers, however, argue that this method would have been too unstable, especially if the builders were using unshaped logs. It is also possible that a ramp could have been made with only two long and flat planks leaning against the uprights. After a 1993 experiment using wooden tracks smeared with grease to transport the stones, an A-frame lever to raise the stones in the hole, and a wooden ramp to drag the lintel on top, engineer Mark Whitby claimed that "With 140 people, I could build Stonehenge for you in less than 20 years."[18] One or more or none of these methods could have actually been used by the Stonehenge builders four thousand years ago; without direct evidence archaeologists are not willing to draw any final conclusions.

An artist's rendition shows how the builders of Stonehenge might have raised the enormous lintels atop the sarsens.

THE SLAUGHTER STONE

Also during the work on Stonehenge IIIa, a huge sarsen called the Slaughter Stone was placed at the left side of the Avenue at the entrance of the embankment, probably as a replacement for a stone set up during Stonehenge I or II. This large, partly smoothed stone 21 feet long, 3 feet thick, and over 7 feet wide now lies on the ground. The surface is bumpy and craggy and stained a rusty red due to rainwater collecting in the holes. Its name was given to it in the eighteenth century when rumors circulated that the Stonehenge people killed humans or animals on this stone before taking them to the Altar Stone as sacrifices to the pagan gods. However, just as archaeologists discovered that the Altar Stone stood upright and was clearly not used in any such manner, they also discerned that the Slaughter Stone once stood upright and functioned as nothing more exciting than one of a pair of stones that marked the entrance. This stone has become a large part of Stonehenge folklore, but as Atkinson points

BUILDING STONEHENGE IN THE SUMMER OF 1993

In 1993, National Geographic Productions hired a team of professionals to attempt a reconstruction of Stonehenge using only the materials and methods available to prehistoric man. The goal was to build the Great Trilithon using concrete blocks that weighed as much as the original stones, a project that involved moving the blocks, digging the holes, securing the two uprights, and raising the lintel on top. When at last the huge trilithon stood raised before them, three of the hundreds of team members shared their excitement in the film documentary "The Secrets of Lost Empires."

Mark Whitby, the project engineer: "These stone age men were pretty ingenious. We've learned an awful lot of respect for them as a result of being handed two forty-ton stones and one nine-ton stone and asked to sort of stand them on their ends and put the nine-ton on top. And I think I've probably gotten nearer to thinking like he might have thought at the time than anybody has for a long time. It's a very nice feeling that it gives you to enter into the soul of somebody as a result of seeing what they've built."

out, "The visitor will listen in vain for the ghostly shrieks of expiring victims spread-eagled on its bloodstained surface, unless he allows his imagination to run well ahead of the facts." [19]

STONEHENGE IIIB (CA. 2000–1550 B.C.)

After 2000 B.C., the sarsen stones remained in place and the only stones that continued to be rearranged at Stonehenge were the bluestones. Construction during Stonehenge IIIb lasted from around 2000 B.C. to around 1550 B.C., and it was during this time that the bluestones were recovered from wherever they had been stored during the Stonehenge IIIa years.

It is unclear what the Stonehenge IIIb builders were trying to achieve with the layout of the bluestones because nothing permanent remains from their efforts. At the very center of the monument, inside of the sarsen horseshoe, they placed approximately 22 of the original bluestones in an oval shape spaced 11 feet apart from each other. At least 2 of the bluestones were made into trilithons because a few bluestones were found with mortises and tenons.

Roger Hopkins, a stonemason from Massachusetts who specializes in moving and shaping granite: "They [the original builders of Stonehenge] were pushing the envelope of their technology. They were taking things that they had seen work and applying them to a massive job that was advancing their technology and by doing so probably advancing their status in their community."

Archaeologist Julian Richards, who at the time had spent fifteen years studying the area around Stonehenge: "We haven't got the final answer yet. We can't say this is how it was done. What we've demonstrated is how it could be done, and we've tried to be as real to the time that Stonehenge was built as possible. Archaeology can answer some questions about Stonehenge, when it was built, something about the society that built it, and this has answered some of the questions about the task, the engineering, how you motivate people, how you organize people, but there's always going to be mystique about Stonehenge."

A few hundred years later, still during Stonehenge IIIb, two concentric circles of holes were dug outside the sarsen circle but were never used as a part of the monument. The purpose of these circles, labeled the Y and Z holes, is still a mystery. It appears that there were 30 holes in each circle, which when added to the 22 set up in an oval inside the horseshoe would have equaled the 82 that were originally brought to the site for the double ring of bluestones planned in Stonehenge II. However, the Y and Z holes were laid out very haphazardly with no signs that bluestones were ever placed in them.

STONEHENGE IIIc (CA. 1550–1100 B.C.)

The building of Stonehenge IIIc, which lasted from around 1550 B.C. to around 1100 B.C., marks the last period in which any stones were rearranged at Stonehenge. At the beginning of this phase, for unknown reasons, the Stonehenge people removed all the bluestones from the oval configuration. They quickly replaced them, though, this time directly inside the sarsen circle. They set up a very uneven circle of bluestones with a diameter of approximately 75 feet, allowing slightly more room on the northeast axis. Scholars are not sure why the circle is so obviously irregular. They agree that it would have been hard to scribe an accurate circle from the center of the henge because the sarsen horseshoe was in the way, but they are not sure why the builders did not simply measure a few feet in from the sarsens in the sarsen circle. Originally there were 60 bluestones in the circle, but today only 6 are still standing, 5 are leaning, 8 have broken or fallen, and 10 are stumps either just above or just below the ground. The rest are missing and were presumably taken in later centuries as building stones. For the most part, the stones in this circle were all left in their natural states rather than shaped or smoothed like the sarsens and lintels.

The rest of the bluestones brought to the site so many centuries before were set up in a horseshoe shape a few feet inside the sarsen horseshoe. These 19 bluestones, unlike the ones in the outer bluestone circle, were all dressed and shaped with their inner faces smoothed. They were cut into either squares or rectangles that tapered slightly toward the top like the sarsens. Like the sarsen horseshoe, the height of the bluestones gradually rises toward the central apex, where the Altar Stone, still a main focus after so many reconstructions, was placed. Unlike

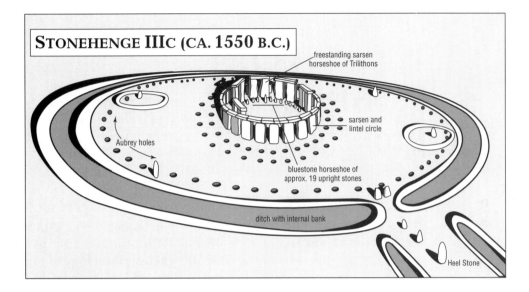

STONEHENGE IIIC (CA. 1550 B.C.)

freestanding sarsen horseshoe of Trilithons

sarsen and lintel circle

Aubrey holes

bluestone horseshoe of approx. 19 upright stones

ditch with internal bank

Heel Stone

the sarsens in the horseshoe, however, these bluestones were not made into trilithons. Only 6 of these are still standing, with a few more in pieces on the ground.

STONEHENGE IV (CA. 1100 B.C.)

Atkinson added a fourth phase to Stonehenge's transformation when it was discovered that many centuries later the Avenue was extended after all building activity within the henge itself had ceased. Another 1½ miles of banks and ditches were created as the Avenue wound its way to the bank of the River Avon at what is now known as West Amesbury. The difficulty in fixing this building activity in any phase is that carbon dating of material found along the Avenue is hard to evaluate. When the builders extended the avenue, there is evidence that they also may have worked on the beginning of the Avenue as well. What this does reveal, however, is that people were still using Stonehenge nearly two thousand years after it was first conceived. What they and their ancestors were using it *for*, however, is a question that people have pondered for centuries.

WHAT WAS THE PURPOSE OF STONEHENGE?

In the absence of written records, the task of figuring out what Stonehenge was used for has fallen to the archaeologists. After a lifetime of studying Stonehenge, Richard Atkinson has a simple, straightforward answer to the Stonehenge question: We do not know, and we shall probably never know. "Most of what has been written about Stonehenge is nonsense or speculation. You can't get at the minds of prehistoric people, who left no written records, except in the most trivial sense. Prehistoric archaeologists can answer only four questions: who? what? when? where? Anyone who purports to answer the question *why* is just bombinating around in the dark [guessing]." [20] Nevertheless, Atkinson was not able to resist adding his own theories to the ever-growing pile.

Based on the discoveries of centuries, dozens of theories have been suggested to explain the unique monument. In every age, new ideas have been advanced, more often based on folktales than on science. The most outrageous theories were usually discarded; some, however, lingered for centuries.

The magician Merlin (pictured) was said to have erected Stonehenge to honor King Arthur's fallen soldiers.

MERLIN AND KING ARTHUR'S UNCLE

In 1136 the medieval chronicler Geoffrey of Monmouth wrote a book entitled *Histories of the Kings of Britain*. He was the first to

THE SOUNDS OF SILENCE

Early-twentieth-century-poet Siegfried Sassoon wrote "The Heart's Journey," his verse contemplation of the ancient ruins of Stonehenge. The poem is taken from Sassoon's *Collected Poems (1908–1956)*.

> What is Stonehenge? It is the roofless past;
> Man's ruinous myth; his uninterred adoring
> Of the unknown in sunrise cold and red;
> His quest of stars that arch his doomed exploring.
>
> And what is Time but shadows that were cast
> By these storm-sculptured stones while centuries fled?
> The stones remain; their stillness can outlast
> The skies of history hurrying overhead.

take on the subject of the origin and purpose of Stonehenge, and his words have remained a main focus of Stonehenge legend. In accordance with the superstitious nature of his society, Geoffrey attributed the moving of the stones to the magic of King Arthur's clever magician, Merlin. The legend states that King Aurelius Ambrosius, Arthur's uncle, wanted to build a monument to his soldiers who had died on Salisbury Plain at the hands of an evil Saxon leader. He enlisted the help of Merlin, who told him about an existing stone circle in Ireland:

> Send for the Giants' Dance [a reference to the belief that the stones were originally giants or even dancing people who were turned into stone for celebrating on the Sabbath] which is on Mount Killaraus in Ireland. In that place there is a stone construction which no man of this period could ever erect, unless he combined great skill and artistry. The stones are enormous, and there is no one alive strong enough to move them. If they are placed in position round this site, in the way they are put up over there, they will stand for ever. Many years ago the Giants transported them from the remotest confines of Africa and set them up in Ireland at a time when they inhabited that country. Their plan was that, whenever they felt ill, baths should be prepared at the foot of the stones for they used to pour water over them and to run this water into baths in which their sick were cured.[21]

Geoffrey relays that when fifteen thousand of the king's men could not move the stones, Merlin magically transported them onto ships, smooth winds carried them to England, and Merlin reset the stones in their Irish pattern. Later, King Aurelius and his brother (Arthur's father) were buried at the center of the ring.

Often at the root of folklore a hint of the truth can be found. In this case, the bluestones were indeed brought from an area on an established trade route between Ireland and Wessex and they were transported to Salisbury Plain partly over water, though not an ocean. Linking the tale with the time of King Arthur, however, is entirely the stuff of legend. That would place the building of Stonehenge at around A.D. 485, nearly two thousand years later than the commonly accepted dates. Even Geoffrey's contemporaries doubted his story. Historian William of Newburgh proclaimed, "It is quite clear that everything this man wrote about Arthur and his successors . . . was made up partly by himself and partly by others, either from an inordinate love of lying, or for the sake of pleasing the Britons." [22] The irrefutable fact is that this legend had a lasting effect on the history of Stonehenge, weaving its way into art, literature, and music since the twelfth century.

English architect Inigo Jones (1573–1652) believed Stonehenge was the work of Roman invaders.

LOOKING FOR OUTSIDE INFLUENCES

No other documented explanations for the monument would supplant the King Arthur story until the seventeenth century, when King James I hired architect Inigo Jones to explore the matter. After surveying Stonehenge, Jones decided that it clearly was a Roman building, built as a dwelling place for the Roman gods. His scholarly background was Roman architecture, and he compared the blueprint of Stonehenge with classical Roman buildings and insisted they were of the same mold. He refused to believe that the native Britons could ever have created such a monument, saying that they were a "savage and barbarous People, knowing no use at all of Garments, and if destitute of the Knowledge, even to clothe themselves, much less any Knowledge had they to erect stately structures, or such remarkable Works as Stone-Heng." [23]

Like Geoffrey's speculations about Merlin, this theory's fatal flaw was the actual date of the construction of Stonehenge. Historians in the late seventeenth century, however, did begin the trend of searching for an outside influence to explain the monument. During this period the Greeks were given credit for building Stonehenge, as were the Phoenicians (with the help of Hercules), the Danes, and even the residents of the lost city of Atlantis. The theory of a Greek or Mediterranean influence was taken most seriously. A carving of a dagger on one of the stones is very similar to a type thought to be used at that time in Minoan Crete and Mycenae, and some of the objects found in nearby graves show a Mediterranean influence or origin. It is now commonly believed that the Stonehenge dagger actually predated the use of similar daggers in Mycenae. Trade routes had certainly been established by the time the large sarsens were being erected, and one must consider the possibility that some knowledge from other societies was spread as well.

THE DRUIDS' CONNECTION TO STONEHENGE

Without a doubt, the most enduring vision of Stonehenge is that of Druids performing celebratory rituals among the stone circles. In the centuries immediately preceding the spread of Christianity in Britain, the Druids were supposedly the priests and lawmakers, doctors and philosophers of the Celtic people. The Celts fiercely opposed the Roman invasion of Britain during these times and believed that to die in battle was the most glorious death possible. Pliny the Elder, the Roman philosopher and writer in the first century A.D., was the first to mention the Druids; it is from him that we know of their existence.

The idea that the Druids were the original builders and overseers of Stonehenge began with John Aubrey in the seventeenth century. In his unpublished work *Templa Druidum*, he claimed he had "clear evidence that these monuments [Stonehenge] were Pagan Temples, which was not made out before, and also, with humble submission to better judgement offered, a probability that they were Temples of the Druids. . . . This inquiry I must confess is a groping in the Dark." [24] At this time in

This nineteenth-century illustration shows Druids worshiping at Stonehenge. The theory that Stonehenge was built by the Druids began in the seventeenth century.

Britain a movement was under way to portray the ancient Britons as less barbaric than the Roman conquerors had made them out to be. The Druids fit the bill and William Stukeley decided to support the Druid theory in the next century, bringing it to the forefront of British thought.

Stukeley's vision of the Druids was rather different from the descriptions that had been passed down from classical accounts. His Druids were joyous seekers of wisdom and goodness rather than eccentrics and barbarians who burned their sacrificial victims alive. John Aubrey, however, thought the native British population brutish and claimed that the ancient Britons were "almost as savage as the beasts whose skins were their only rayment . . . 2 or 3 degrees I suppose less savage than the Americans." [25] Both images of the Druids have become mixed up in the art and literature on the subject.

The Druids were known to be practicing in Britain by around 250 B.C. and then disappeared until 1781, when a group of men formed the Ancient Order of Druids. Different factions formed, all based on different aspects of what writers over the centuries have attributed to Druids, often creating a hodgepodge of rules, practices, and beliefs. In the early twentieth century Druids began performing rituals and celebrating the summer solstice at Stonehenge and they have remained a common sight among the ruins.

DISPROVING THE DRUID CONNECTION TO STONEHENGE

Stonehenge predates by thousands of years the Druids' appearance in British history, and there is no evidence that the two were ever connected. Furthermore, every mention of the ancient Druids indicates that they held their meetings and rituals in groves of oak trees or caves, not in man-made buildings or open fields. Nevertheless, modern-day Druids insist that their ancient predecessors were an integral part of the activities at Stonehenge.

The Roman invaders may have thought so too. In A.D. 61 they ranged the countryside destroying pagan sites where groups like the Druids were thought to worship. When they got to Stonehenge, they only ruined part of it. Perhaps they decided the stones were too heavy to bother with or faced the probability that the Druids had nothing to do with the monument; regardless, they decided not to completely destroy it. Modern-day Druids believe that the fact that the Romans damaged Stonehenge may have actually driven the Druids there in an act of defiance against Roman oppression.

Modern-day Druids claim that clear evidence of Druidic occupation at Stonehenge was stolen or lost during an excavation in the seventeenth century by the duke of Buckingham. Secular Arch Druid Tim Sebastian maintains that the duke "desecrated the center of Stonehenge, where many items were dug up and stolen; they included precious metal Druidic ritual ornaments, a golden cape of an Arch Druid and a ritual silver-tipped ram's horn."[26] Unfortunately the duke's records of this find were vague, and the objects he did mention—bull horns, antlers, stone mauls, and arrowheads—could have been those he found in a nearby burial mound. Regardless of the real relationship between the Druids and Stonehenge in ancient times, the connection remains strong today, even as the search for other explanations continues.

"ALTERNATIVE ARCHAEOLOGY"

Alternative archaeologists are enthusiastic men and women who develop their own theories and explanations about ancient sites through means other than professional excavation. They maintain a belief in "the existence in prehistoric times of an active science of spiritual physics, whereby the functions of mind and body were integrated with currents in the earth and powers from the cosmos." [27] Their approaches and beliefs are considered unorthodox by most professional archaeologists who have studied Stonehenge, but these dedicated groups thrive in today's society.

One subject much discussed by alternative archaeologists is the link between Stonehenge and aliens. UFOs have been reported hovering over Stonehenge and nearby areas for years. Strange lights and apparitions have been sighted near the stones and John Michell, a well-known alternative thinker, believes that Stonehenge may be a life-size model of an actual flying saucer built to attract the real thing. Michell also believes that Stonehenge is actually a reflection of the biblical Garden of Eden, which he deduced through mathematics and numerology. He claims that the dimensions of the sarsen circle symbolize and model the dimensions of the earth so that anyone studying the layout of Stonehenge will be able to garner important information about the world. Other researchers have taken that idea further and conclude that Stonehenge is actually a miniature model of the solar system, with the long barrows representing the constellations.

Robe-clad Druids observe the rites of their summer solstice celebration in this 1973 photo.

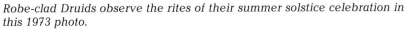

LEY-LINES

Alternative archaeologists are most keenly interested not in UFOlogy or numerology, however, but in the study of ley-lines. The concept of ley-lines is based on the theory that many (if not all) of prehistoric, pagan, and megalithic sites around the world are linked by a series of straight lines that ancient man purposefully constructed. The existence of ley-lines and the whole field of "earth mysteries" has been hotly debated by archaeologists and other scientists. According to Aubrey Burl, a highly respected expert on prehistoric stone circles, "The most lunatic ideas about prehistoric monuments is that of ley-lines. These are fabrications of the twentieth century, invented by Alfred Watkins in the 1920s." [28] What Watkins theorized was that trade routes and travelers' networks in the Neolithic period were set up along these postulated straight lines. However, a close look at the Stonehenge ley-line supposed to connect it with an earthwork at Old Sarum, Salisbury Cathedral, and a hill fort at Clearbury Rings reveals that traders would have had to cross four rivers, wade through a swamp, and then cross another river to reach the four sites, which do not actually connect on a straight line at all. Historians believe it is highly unlikely that any traders would have taken such a roundabout route to their destination.

A big problem many people have with the concept of ley-lines is that they supposedly link sites that are from radically different time periods or that served entirely different functions. Proponents argue that a Christian church built in the medieval period can be a valid spot on a prehistoric ley-line because the church probably was built over an ancient site that was situated along the line. Controversy aside, the study of ley-lines continues to thrive today, although the focus has shifted a bit. "Ley hunters," as they call themselves, search for ancient ley-lines that they believe served a much higher purpose than to simply denote trade routes. They believe that the lines trace a pathway of energy that links megalithic or other seemingly pagan ritual sites, forming a pattern of magnetic forces. Ley hunters have tested many stone sites and believe they have found strong magnetic fields surrounding some of the huge stones. A technique known as dowsing has been used in their investigations. In dowsing a person gently holds two dowsing rods, usually made of metal, and slowly approaches the area to be tested. The reaction of the rods supposedly indicates strengthening or

UNDER THE MISTLETOE

The first century A.D. Roman writer Pliny the Elder's only surviving work is a thirty-seven-volume encyclopedia of the natural sciences, *Historia naturalis (Natural History)*. Modern historians have learned much about the ancient world from this invaluable source. Pliny may have been the first writer to associate the Druids with oak trees, forest groves, and mistletoe.

> The Druids hold nothing more sacred than the mistletoe and the tree on which it grows, provided it is an oak. They choose the oak to form groves, and they do not perform any religious rites without its foliage. . . . Anything growing on those trees they regard as sent from heaven and a sign that this tree has been chosen by the gods themselves. Mistletoe is, however, very rarely found, and when found, it is gathered with great ceremony and especially on the sixth day of the moon. . . . They prepare a ritual sacrifice and feast under the tree, and lead up two white bulls whose horns are bound for the first time on this occasion. A priest attired in a white vestment ascends the tree and with a golden pruning hook cuts the mistletoe which is caught in a white cloth. Then next they sacrifice the victims praying that the gods will make their gifts propitious to those to whom

weakening of the magnetic pull in the area. Dowsing has been used since ancient times to search for water or certain minerals running beneath the surface of the earth. In the case of Stonehenge, one experienced dowser believes he found incredibly strong magnetic fields radiating from Stonehenge at intervals of approximately 30 degrees at a height of eight feet above the ground. Dowsing has also located springs of water running underneath the stones radiating out from the center of the henge.

These findings have led some to conclude that Stonehenge is a "beacon" that collects and rechannels the earth's energy to other important sites. It would have been built by people who, according to alternative archaeologists, were more in touch with nature and could detect and harness these energy patterns. What they would have done with this power is unclear, and some researchers have turned to the patterns of the stones themselves for more answers.

A Druidic priest cuts the sacred mistletoe from a tree while Roman soldiers look on.

they have given it. They believe that if given in drink the mistletoe will give fecundity to any barren animal, and that it is predominant against all poisons.

STONEHENGE AS ANCIENT OBSERVATORY AND CALENDAR

The most pervasive twentieth-century theory concerning Stonehenge is the notion that the megaliths were set up to serve as a calendar or an ancient computer to predict astronomical events. It had long been noted that the thirty sarsens in the circle might symbolize the days of the month, and the nineteen bluestones in the horseshoe could represent the nineteen-year cycle of the moon. But the notion that these representations could have been more than just symbolic has been explored only relatively recently.

The astronomical interpretation of Stonehenge was popularized by Gerald Hawkins, an English astronomer who lived and worked in America, and was modified soon after by another astronomer, Fred Hoyle. In 1965 Hawkins published a book on the subject titled *Stonehenge Decoded* and set off a rousing debate among archaeologists and astronomers. Armed

THE RUINS OF STONEHENGE

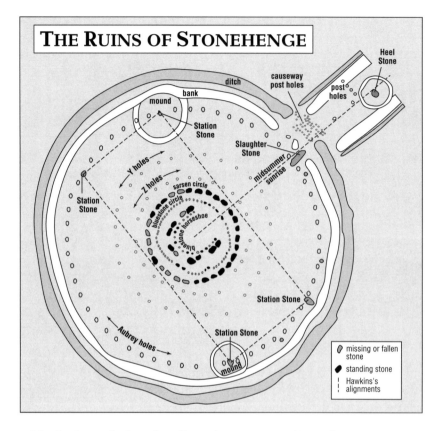

with the knowledge that Stonehenge was aligned on the axis of the midsummer sunrise and midwinter sunset, Hawkins revived and expanded upon the idea that the sarsen stones were laid out to identify the change of the seasons according to which stones sunlight struck. He also claimed to find alignments of the sun and the moon in Stonehenge I that could not possibly be coincidental. But the real controversy came from his claim that the 56 Aubrey holes around the inner bank of Stonehenge were actually used to plot the positions of the sun and moon. This, in effect, would allow the Stonehenge people to predict eclipses of the moon, which occur every 18.61 years. That number multiplied by 3 can be rounded to 56, which Hawkins believes means the 56 Aubrey holes were created for this reason. With the movements of the heavens as their only calendar, predicting the eclipses would have been valuable in a society that would fear sudden darkness in the daytime sky. Using an IBM computer, Hawkins first entered the known movements of the moon in the sky over Stonehenge in 1554 B.C. He then calculated what would happen if small stones were placed inside specific Aubrey holes. He discovered that if the builders had placed stones in specific holes and moved them every year, when the stone landed in Hole 56, in front of the Heel Stone, an eclipse would occur. Hoyle modified this approach a few years later to make the system more accurate. Many remained unconvinced. According to Atkinson, "Hawkins' book is one of the worst ever written. It's not a loony book; it was written by someone who purports to be an astronomer. Shocking! He sent me the manuscript, and I sent back five . . . pages, single-spaced on both sides, simply listing errors." [29]

Inaccuracies aside, carbon dating done after Hawkins's research pushed the time that the Aubrey holes were in use back to around 2800 B.C., when the earth's axis and the schedule of eclipses would have been different than those Hawkins used for his calculations. Furthermore, some of the Aubrey holes were

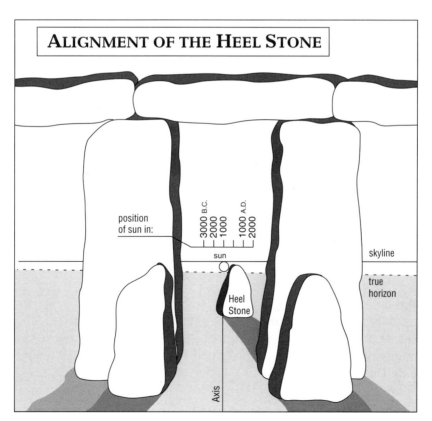

ALIGNMENT OF THE HEEL STONE

position of sun in:

3000 B.C.
2000
1000
1000 A.D.
2000

sun

skyline

true horizon

Heel Stone

Axis

covered over by the Station Stones early on in Stonehenge's history, which would have made this elaborate system no longer feasible. Doubters of the "calendar/observatory" theory argue that when any circular object (even a wagon wheel) is placed on the ground there will be correlations between the spokes and the patterns of the constellations. Their point is that it would be remarkable if something *did not* match up at Stonehenge. Scholars are willing to accept that there may be some validity to the "Neolithic observatory" idea, but most are unwilling to accept it as the final answer.

STONEHENGE AS A MULTIPURPOSE SITE

Christopher Chippindale, a British archaeologist, has studied nearly everything ever written or suggested about Stonehenge and concludes only that it must have been a temple of some sort: "We do not know exactly what was worshipped at Stonehenge. We do not know if everyone in the community went to it, or only a special few men or women or children or old people. We do not know if worshippers entered it in joy or terror. We do not know if worship filled their lives or meant their deaths. But we do know that Stonehenge was a religious place, a sacred site." [30]

Over the many centuries that Stonehenge was in use it likely served a multitude of different functions, from the sacred to the mundane. A temple for worshiping a variety of gods; a meeting hall; a court for dispensing justice; a marketplace for trading and selling goods; a cemetery; an elaborate timekeeping device—all of these uses are quite possible. Some of the more "creative" theories of why Stonehenge was built—as a beacon to harness and distribute the sun's energy around the earth, as a landing site for UFOs, or to cover a mysteriously appearing crop circle thought to be a sacred space created by the gods—keep researchers and archaeologists on their toes, and exemplify the imagination of modern society. As famed archaeologist Jacquetta Hawkes wrote in *Antiquity* magazine, every age has the Stonehenge it deserves—or desires.

After centuries of destruction and mistreatment, England now faces the tough job of ensuring that Stonehenge is protected. Otherwise, future generations may not get the chance to stand before it and wonder what it was all about. And in all probability, new discoveries about the world's greatest stone monument and new ideas about its meaning are still waiting to be hatched.

DESTRUCTION, RESTORATION, AND PRESERVATION

Who actually owns a structure as ancient as Stonehenge? Who is responsible for protecting it? These questions have been a source of great confusion and disagreement over the last few centuries. From the Middle Ages, Stonehenge belonged to whoever owned the fields of the Amesbury estate on which the monument stood. The owners could then do with the monument as they pleased. From the seventeenth century on, a clear lineage of owners can be traced. These men included Sir Lawrence Washington, an ancestor of the first president of the United States.

For the next two hundred years, the owners managed the monument in various ways—some banned historians and archaeologists from the site, others were more accommodating. One owner bred a colony of rabbits among the stones, then held an annual fair at the site. Another dug out the rabbits, and propped up some leaning stones. At one point a refreshment stand was built in the center of the monument and a large trench was dug out of the ground to store wine. In 1898 the nephew of longtime proprietor Edmund Antrobus inherited the estate and put Stonehenge up for sale at an exorbitant price. When no buyers turned up, he built the first wire fence around the stones and charged admission to visitors. In 1915 the Amesbury estate was divided and sold at auction. Cecil Chubb, a local landowner, purchased the portion of the grounds that Stonehenge occupied because his wife wanted it. In 1918 Chubb donated the monument to the government. Stonehenge is now an official World Heritage Site, along with the Pyramids of Egypt, the Grand Canyon, and the Taj Mahal in India. This special designation means that the whole world shares the responsibility for and ownership of the monument. In practical terms, the stones themselves and the thirteen acres they stand on

Stonehenge was privately owned until 1918, when then-owner Cecil Chubb donated it to the British government. It is now a World Heritage Site.

are under the guardianship of the English Heritage Foundation, and the fifteen hundred acres surrounding the monument are owned by the National Trust. Together, these government agencies are charged with ensuring an end to the destruction that has taken place there and preserving the stones for the future.

WHY STONEHENGE IS NOW A RUIN

After more than four thousand years, much less than half of Stonehenge is still standing. Knowing some stones have withstood the passage of time has led researchers to wonder why the rest have not. Piecing together how it was destroyed is not an easy task. Most of the destruction took place before records of the site were kept, so scientists can identify only stones that fell or were taken away in the last few centuries. Sometimes the only way to tell that something occurred was by comparing two artists' drawings of the site. The presence of a stone in one but not another allowed scientists to narrow the date of the removal of that stone. Basically, the destruction of Stonehenge was the work of both man and nature, sometimes in tandem.

Salisbury Plain has endured heavy storms and high winds over the many centuries that Stonehenge has stood, and the weather clearly took its toll on the stones and on the already weak foundation beneath them. The stones on the southwest side of the monument bore the brunt of gale-force winds that may have caused the stones to shift in their sockets and eventually to fall. Many centuries of the ground freezing, thawing, and then freezing again would also have loosened the stones in their foundations.

Furthermore, the weather can be held partly responsible for causing severe wear and tear on the faces of the stones, leaving them dull in color and rougher than when they were erected. It took mankind, however, to destroy the monument on a grand scale.

BUT HAROLD, IT'S SO DINKY!

In her *Discover* magazine article "Stonehenge: Can It Be Saved?" author Gina Maranto gives this description of visiting modern-day Stonehenge.

> On a sunny summer day when a mob of tourists descends on it, visiting England's best known example of Neolithic architecture is about as inspiring as shopping at Bloomingdale's on Christmas Eve. You drive around the parking lot, and then the overflow parking lot, for ten, fifteen minutes, waiting for a slot; navigate through the loitering crowds of sightseers licking their prepackaged Walls Ice Cream cones; pay your 1 pound entrance fee; trudge through the concrete tunnel under A344, come up wham-bam on the north side of Stonehenge, and make a disappointing circuit fifty yards from the stones, peering to make out details and trying hard to ignore the reedy voice of some fubsy matron from Boca Raton declaiming at the top of her lungs, "But it's so dinky, Harold. Why is it so dinky?"

DESTRUCTION AT THE HANDS OF MEN

The human destruction of Stonehenge most likely first began with the Roman invasions of England in the first century A.D. In the following centuries, many megalithic structures around Europe were pulled down because they were considered pagan, not Christian, and reminders of civilizations conquered. In medieval times the stones were stolen by stonemasons and peasants to make bridges and houses. Local farmers would set fires right next to the stones in an attempt to make them crack. They would then carry large chunks away and use them for building stones. In the early fourteenth century, at a time when stone circles became associated with witches, many of the stones were pulled down or shattered for superstitious reasons.

Furthermore, until fairly recently, visitors to the site were allowed free rein to wander through the stones and even to climb upon them. Continual touching has left some of the stone faces uneven, smooth in spots and rough in others, while climbing on the stones for centuries with hard shoes has scratched the surfaces. Victorian tourists would picnic amid the stones on summer days, leaving behind "a good scatter of picnic remains,

WAITING FOR BETTER DAYS

Writer John Fowles laments the present-day ruin in *The Enigma of Stonehenge.*

Stonehenge has done sterling service in aid of the imagination, and I think it is time the native imagination did a little more to repay the debt than offering it mere physical protection. The old pastoral setting of before this century is gone for ever and cannot return. Today is crowds, cars, coaches, lavatories, shops. . . . All skeleton, no heart. We can never regain the old landscape or the emotional effect of the old monument, just as a wild animal in a zoo can never effectively resemble the wild animal in its natural habitat. Only a very few now, the fortunate archaeologist, the fortunate photographer, can hope to have a glimpse of it. The rest of us must stay as imprisoned, as rejected, as the stones themselves; and like them, can only stand and wait for better days.

Tourists wander around Stonehenge in 1966. Until recently, people were allowed to touch the stones and even climb on them.

broken bottles, dirty papers, chicken and chop bones, and what the Victorians called 'litter,' horse dung and straw soaked in horse piss." [31] Putting credence in the legends of the magical or healthful powers of the stones, visitors were fond of taking hammers and chiseling off pieces to use for medicines or in teas or baths. Encyclopedist Benjamin Martin wrote in 1755 that "Great Injury has been done to these Stones by the unaccountable Folly of Mankind in breaking Pieces off with great Hammers." [32] He apparently could not resist the urge himself, because he then writes that it took him forty-five minutes of hammering just to get an ounce and a half of stone. John Aubrey explains that he witnessed many local people hammering at the stones because they believed that "pieces, or powder, of these stones put into their wells, do drive away the toads, with which their wells are much infested." [33] Even the great antiquarian William Stukeley was guilty of treating the stones a bit shabbily. One day he and a companion used a ladder to climb to the top of a trilithon to

Stonehenge has been plagued with graffiti throughout its history. Here, a spray-painted message demonstrates one of the newer forms of graffiti.

enjoy the view from there. He recorded that he had not realized half of the wonder of the place until he stood high above it. In fact, he and his friends even dined while sitting aloft and left their pipes behind when they finished. Well into the nineteenth century people continued to take pieces of the stones as souvenirs, and the nearby hotels accommodated them by offering hammers for rent.

DESTRUCTION IN THE TWENTIETH CENTURY

Graffiti has always been a part of Stonehenge, and nearly all of the sarsens have at least one name or set of initials etched into them. This tradition continued in the twentieth century, but in arguably more damaging fashion. "Spray [paint] a message on the stones and you're guaranteed media coverage,"[34] said one of the security guards who now patrol the area. In 1961 someone painted BAN THE BOMB in large yellow letters across the sarsens in the outer circle, and various banners and signs have been posted over the stones espousing an assortment of causes. The paint is always quickly removed by a process that strips away more of the precious stone.

Throughout most of the twentieth century, the English Ministry of Defense has used the area around Stonehenge for military training, maneuvers, and weapons testing. Soldiers actually set up a base right next to the stones during World War I and rumor has it that "a local airfield commander wanted to remove the megaliths entirely because they presented a danger to low-flying planes." [35] Even today an army base is only a mile from Stonehenge and the military is blamed for disturbing or destroying approximately 350 ancient earthworks and burial mounds in the area.

While fairs and gatherings were held amid the stones in centuries past, nothing rivaled the Stonehenge People's Free Festival that was held every summer from 1974 to 1984. The huge festivals drew musicians, fans, motorcycle gangs, and groups of people who roamed England in their campers. In 1984, thirty thousand people descended on the site, many building temporary dwellings and camping there throughout the summer. The attendees dug holes for bathrooms and electric generators and rode their motorcycles over burial mounds. Political activists set the portable latrines on fire, and warring gangs set each other's cars and campers on fire and then left them behind when they finally departed. Local taxpayers were forced to clean up the damage at a cost of over £120,000 (roughly $190,000).

Besides detracting from the beauty of Stonehenge, many fear that environmental pollution from two nearby highways is damaging the stones and the ground itself. More than twenty thousand cars and trucks speed by daily on the A303, a major highway only one hundred yards from the stones. A smaller road, the A344, passes only inches from the Heel Stone and cuts straight through the Avenue. Some fear that the vibrations of passing trucks will loosen the stones in their foundations, even though most of the stones have been reinforced to prevent them from shifting.

RESTORING STONEHENGE

Restoring Stonehenge to its original glory is virtually impossible; the maxim that "Restoration is a lie" is held by most historians and antiquarians. To these purists, an ancient monument rebuilt by modern man detracts from its authenticity. Compromises were first made at Stonehenge by allowing geologists to strengthen the structure to avoid more damage. Work began in

1901 under the careful supervision of William Gowland and a noted architect. The one remaining sarsen of the largest trilithon still standing was leaning at a precarious 60-degree angle and posed a threat to nearby stones. A wooden cradle protected the stone while Gowland carefully excavated around the base. A concrete foundation was poured to replace the naturally weak chalk foundation and the stone was slowly pulled upright. It was from this project that Gowland gained valuable information about how the stone was originally raised. Other stones that were leaning less severely were propped up with wooden poles, and in 1919 more stones were straightened and cemented in place. Gowland was too old at this point to supervise, so the job went to famed archaeologist Arthur Evans. The leaning stones were all topped by lintels that had to be taken down before the uprights were straightened. Each lintel was wrapped in felt and then encased in a wooden frame and hoisted off the uprights. When the uprights were straight and secure again, each lintel was securely reattached.

From this point on, the only restoration of Stonehenge would be to raise stones that had fallen in recent recorded history. In 1958, Atkinson and Piggott supervised the lifting of sarsens that had fallen in 1797 and in 1900. This time the stones were encased in steel cages padded with felt and a sixty-ton crane was required to lift them. They were then carefully maneuvered into new concrete foundations. Five years later another sarsen in the circle fell, most likely as a result of a jarring it sustained during the 1958 restoration. It was put back up, and concrete was added to the foundations of more stones, leaving only seven sarsens still in their original chalk foundations today.

PRESERVING STONEHENGE

Once the stones had been strengthened in the ground, the question was how to protect and preserve the monument for the future. One Cambridge archaeologist recommended closing the monument to everyone except bona fide scholars. Even Atkinson said that "if preservation is your goal, then the monument must not be polluted by visitors. If that means you restrict who can get close, well then, all right." [36] Unwilling to resort to these drastic measures, the government took small steps to protect the site. The ground inside the circle was covered with gravel in an effort to protect the soil, which tended to turn into a swamp

To protect and preserve Stonehenge, the English government has taken measures to prevent soil erosion and further damage to the stones by tourists.

when trampled upon in the rain. This only led to more scuffing of the stones, however, and in 1978 the turf was replaced and the Department of the Environment roped off the area around the stones to prevent further damage. A schedule limited visitation to certain days, usually closely monitored by guards.

THE BATTLE OF THE BEANFIELD

In 1985 the English Heritage Foundation and the National Trust canceled what would have been the 11th People's Free Festival as well as the Druids' summer solstice ceremony to avoid the widespread destruction caused by concertgoers the previous year. More than a thousand police officers set up blockades on the streets and wired off the fields. A caravan of 150 vehicles arrived anyway, determined to reach Stonehenge and hold their

People gather at the edge of the barbed-wire fence around Stonehenge for a 1985 summer solstice party. Partygoers later clashed with the police officers who attempted to disperse them.

festival. They were stopped at a nearby beanfield. According to one reporter, "What followed next was a scene that was part *Monty Python*, part *Road Warrior*. Trucks and motor homes careered around the field aiming to knock the policemen down, while the police ran after them throwing rocks and trying to smash their windshields."[37] Serious violence erupted, 420 people were arrested, nearby homes were looted and trashed, and the police were charged with undue brutality. A direct result of this incident, the Public Order Act of 1986 restricted the number of vehicles that could legally travel or park together in England to twelve. A new trespassing ban also was created at this time limiting the number of people who could legally walk in a procession, ensuring that guards at Stonehenge will not be overpowered again. A four-mile, four-day exclusion zone was set up around the monument over the period of the summer solstice, which meant that all visitors had to stay at least four miles away from the stones during that time. The ban was strictly enforced by guards patrolling the area twenty-four hours a day. The English Heritage Foundation issued a report assuring people it had Stonehenge's best interests at heart: "The commission's first aim is preservation. Its second is to make a visit to Stonehenge both aesthetically and intellectually satisfying by drawing attention not just to the monument but also to the surrounding downs." [38] Regardless of the restrictions and the controversy, however, there is no lack of visitors to the site.

STONEHENGE, THE TOURIST ATTRACTION

Off the A344 is a large parking lot that is filled with tour buses and rental cars every day of the week except for December 24 through 26. There is a small admission fee to the site, a complimentary audio tour in six languages, a visitors center and gift shop, a cafeteria, and a baby-changing facility. There is a local Stonehenge museum in Salisbury and another in nearby Devizes for visitors who really want to learn about the history of the site and the people who inhabited the region so long ago. Unfortunately, many people skip these educational journeys, and the average tourist only stays at the stones for a mere thirty minutes, just enough time to snap a few pictures and buy a postcard. When they disembark from their cars and buses, they purchase tickets and head through an underground pedestrian tunnel that leads to the monument itself. A clear path is laid out around the roped-off stones and visitors are encouraged to follow trails through the surrounding fields to see the burial mounds. After a recent visit writer John Fowles noted that "the dominant sound is not the larksong of my [childhood] memory, but the rather less poetic territorial whine of the long-distance truck. . . . Conservation is a fine thing, yet one feels in some way cheated of a birthright." [39]

Many visitors complain that the sacred atmosphere of the place has been replaced by refreshment stands and cheesy souvenirs. People are further frustrated by their inability to walk freely among the stones as in ages past. To address these problems, the English Heritage Foundation has tried for many years to develop a plan that would bring back the natural beauty of the site without compromising the safety of the stones.

For years plans to improve the current situation at Stonehenge have been tied up in political red tape. A joint committee of the English Heritage Foundation and the National Trust makes new suggestions to the government, with four main guiding principles governing any changes or additions: minimum damage to known or potential archaeological remains; minimum impact on previously undeveloped landscape; minimum visual intrusion on monuments and landscape; and maximum reversibility at the end of their usefulness.

The first proposal to be given serious consideration was to reroute the two busy roads farther away from the monument. This would both simplify the congested traffic problems and grant needed space for an improved visitors center. Engineers were consulted about the possibility of running the roads in a tunnel underground so that at least part of them would be unseen. This idea was viewed as promising until the Transport Ministry determined the huge expense of such an undertaking and the environmental problems it might bring. Another suggestion was made to widen the existing roads, which would indeed improve the flow of traffic but would cause even more damage to the archaeologically rich landscape.

Debate continues as new road plans are regularly proposed and rejected. Meanwhile, the local citizens are doing their best to protect the land and the stones. The military base that shares the Stonehenge landscape is making up for past sins by paying more attention to the land its troops trample. The English Heritage Foundation and other concerned parties search for more ways to save, improve, and preserve Stonehenge.

THE SAVE STONEHENGE CAMPAIGN

An early proposition to pacify those clamoring for the right to walk among the stones was to build a fiberglass or styrofoam model out of sight of the original. This life-size replica of Stonehenge, nicknamed "Foamhenge," would give people an appreciation of the size and layout of the stones without causing further damage to the real stones. But the proposal for Foamhenge was quickly squelched by widespread public mockery.

Meanwhile, until the trip to the real Stonehenge is improved for visitors, the English Heritage Foundation and computer chip manufacturer Intel launched a virtual reality model of Stonehenge on the Internet. On a three-dimensional self-guided tour of the stones, users can go back and forth in time to observe the different stages of construction and view the stones from different angles and at different times of the day. This interactive, educational site demonstrates the English Heritage Foundation's commitment to giving people an understanding and appreciation of Stonehenge, even from thousands of miles away in the comfort of their own home.

Finally, as part of their Save Stonehenge campaign, the English Heritage Foundation has applied for a £32 million grant to turn the land around Stonehenge into a large park by the end of the twentieth century. This park, known as Millennium Park, will allow visitors who come to the site to see it as it deserves to be seen. The four-thousand-acre park would be partially paid for out of government lottery revenues and would, according to its supporters, "remove the existing disgraceful [parking lot] and visitor center and all the 20th century clutter and would allow the construction of a first-class center capable of handling the 1.5 million visitors that the site is expected to attract annually within 2 decades." [40] The park would clear the approach to the stones so that they would once again appear isolated in the fields, as the builders intended. Visitors might have to walk as far as a mile to reach the stones, but they would gain a better understanding of Stonehenge in the context of the landscape and burial mounds that surround it.

THE STONEHENGE OF THE IMAGINATION

Every visitor sees something different when they go to Stonehenge. To some the stones are smaller than expected, to some they are larger. Some no doubt envision a team of prehistoric men working for weeks to smooth one side of a stone; others hear the music of the ancient Druids. Author John Fowles believes there are actually two Stonehenges,

> the one in stone and the one in the mind. . . . It is not quite like any other ancient monument in these [British] islands, or anywhere else in the world, and that is not because of its physical self and archaeological features, though they are remarkable enough, but because of its power to challenge the imagination of its beholders. Still today it is not what we know of Stonehenge that haunts us, but what we do not and shall never know. It is like some very ancient and corrupt text, of which one can decipher just enough to be sure it is very important, but never enough to establish exactly what it is saying.[41]

Notes

Introduction

1. Quoted in Christopher Chippindale, *Stonehenge Complete.* Ithaca, NY: Cornell University Press, 1983.
2. Quoted in Thomas Arnold, ed., *Henrici Archidiaconi Huntendunensis Historia Anglorum.* Rolls series. Harlow: Longman and Trubner, 1879.

Chapter 1: Early Stonehenge: The Building Site

3. R. J. C. Atkinson, *Stonehenge.* New York: Penguin Books, 1979.
4. Quoted in Chippindale, *Stonehenge Complete.*
5. Quoted in Stephen Fay, "Close Encounter of a New Kind," *Condé Nast Traveler*, February 1995.
6. Chippindale, *Stonehenge Complete.*
7. Hermann Folkerzheimer, letter to Josiah Simler, August 13, 1562, in Hastings Robinson, ed., *The Zurich Letters*, Second series. London: Parker Society, 1845.
8. Rodney Castleden, *The Making of Stonehenge.* London: Routledge, 1993.
9. E. C. Fernie, "Stonehenge as Architecture," *Art History*, June 1994.
10. Quoted in D. Trull, "Buttered Stonehenge"; available from www.parascope.com/en/stonehng.htm; Internet.
11. Quoted in "The Secrets of Lost Empire," *NOVA*, National Geographic Productions, PBS documentary, 1993.
12. Atkinson, *Stonehenge.*

Chapter 2: Early Stages of Construction

13. Quoted in Chippindale, *Stonehenge Complete.*
14. Quoted in Chippindale, *Stonehenge Complete.*
15. Quoted in Gina Maranto, "Stonehenge: Can It Be Saved?" *Discover*, December 1995.
16. Franklyn M. Branley, *The Mystery of Stonehenge.* New York: Thomas Y. Crowell, 1969.

Chapter 3: Later Stages of Construction

17. Atkinson, *Stonehenge.*
18. Quoted in Stephen Fay, "How They Built Stonehenge," *Reader's Digest*, December 1996.
19. Atkinson, *Stonehenge.*

Chapter 4: What Was the Purpose of Stonehenge?

20. Quoted in Maranto, "Stonehenge: Can It Be Saved?"
21. Quoted in Chippindale, *Stonehenge Complete.*
22. Quoted in Chippindale, *Stonehenge Complete.*
23. Quoted in Chippindale, *Stonehenge Complete.*
24. Quoted in John Fowles, *The Enigma of Stonehenge.* New York: Summit Books, 1980.
25. John Aubrey, "An essay towards the description of the north division of Wiltshire," quoted in Michael Hunter, *John Aubrey and the Realm of Learning.* London: Duckworth, 1975.
26. Quoted in Christopher Chippindale et al., *Who Owns Stonehenge?* London: B. T. Batsford, 1990.
27. Paul Screeton, *Quicksilver Heritage.* London: Thorsons, 1974.
28. Aubrey Burl, *Rings of Stone.* New York: Ticknor & Fields, 1980.
29. Quoted in Maranto, "Stonehenge: Can It Be Saved?"
30. Christopher Chippindale et al., "The Mystery of Stonehenge," *UNESCO Courier*, November 1990.

Chapter 5: Destruction, Restoration, and Preservation

31. Quoted in Chippindale, *Stonehenge Complete.*
32. Quoted in Fowles, *The Enigma of Stonehenge.*
33. Quoted in Castleden, *The Making of Stonehenge.*
34. Quoted in Fay, "Close Encounter of a New Kind."
35. Maranto, "Stonehenge: Can It Be Saved?"
36. Quoted in Maranto, "Stonehenge: Can It Be Saved?"
37. Maranto, "Stonehenge: Can It Be Saved?"
38. Quoted in Maranto, "Stonehenge: Can It Be Saved?"
39. Fowles, *The Enigma of Stonehenge.*
40. Quoted in Richard W. Stevenson, "Saving Stonehenge: A Victim of Success," *New York Times*, February 4, 1996.
41. Fowles, *The Enigma of Stonehenge.*

FOR FURTHER READING

R. J. C. Atkinson, *Stonehenge*. New York: Penguin Books, 1979.

Franklyn M. Branley, *The Mystery of Stonehenge*. New York: Thomas Y. Crowell, 1969.

Aubrey Burl, *Rings of Stone*. New York: Ticknor & Fields, 1980.

Rodney Castleden, *The Making of Stonehenge*. London: Routledge, 1993.

Christopher Chippindale, *Stonehenge Complete*. Ithaca, NY: Cornell University Press, 1983.

John Fowles, *The Enigma of Stonehenge*. New York: Summit Books, 1980.

Websites:

English Heritage Foundation: http://www.uk-guide.com/s-west /stonehen.htm

Stonehenge Information and Links: http://home.earthlink.net /~shadowfax/sfstone.htm

http://www.vivanet.com/~caswell/wilts/stonheng.htm

Virtual Stonehenge: http://connectedpc/com/cpc/ecs/stonehenge/

WORKS CONSULTED

Thomas Arnold, ed., *Henrici Archidiaconi Huntendunensis Historia Anglorum*. Rolls series. Harlow: Longman and Trubner, 1879.

John Aubrey, "An essay towards the description of the north division of Wiltshire," in Michael Hunter, *John Aubrey and the Realm of Learning*. London: Duckworth, 1975.

Aubrey Burl, *The Stonehenge People*. London: J. M. Dent, 1987.

Christopher Chippindale et al., "The Mystery of Stonehenge," *UNESCO Courier*, November 1990.

———, *Who Owns Stonehenge?* London: B. T. Batsford, 1990.

Patrick Crampton, *Stonehenge of the Kings*. New York: John Day, 1967.

Richard R. Doornek, "Stonehenge," *School Arts*, January 1989.

Stephen Fay, "Close Encounter of a New Kind," *Condé Nast Traveler*, February 1995.

———, "How They Built Stonehenge," *Reader's Digest*, December 1996.

E. C. Fernie, "Stonehenge as Architecture," *Art History*, June 1994.

Hermann Folkerzheimer, letter to Josiah Simler, August 13, 1562, in Hastings Robinson, ed., *The Zurich Letters*. Second series. London: Parker Society, 1845.

Gina Maranto, "Stonehenge: Can It Be Saved?" *Discover*, December 1995.

"Midsummer Follies," *Economist*, June 22, 1991.

Cullen Murphy, "The Longest Day," *Atlantic Monthly*, June 1987.

Pliny, *Historia naturalis* 16.95 (Loeb Classical Library, vol. 8, no. 418). Cambridge, MA: Harvard University Press, 1975.

Paul Screeton, *Quicksilver Heritage*. London: Thorsons, 1974.

"The Secrets of Lost Empire," *NOVA*, National Geographic Productions, PBS documentary, 1993.

Richard W. Stevenson, "Saving Stonehenge: A Victim of Success," *New York Times*, February 4, 1996.

"Stonehenge Blues," *Discover*, October 1990.

D. Trull, "Buttered Stonehenge"; available from www.parascope.com/en/stonehng.htm; Internet.

INDEX

aliens (extraterrestrial beings), 66
Altar Stone, 44, 58
Amesbury estate, 73
Ancient Order of Druids, 64
Antrobus, Edmund, 73
archaeology
  alternative, 65–67, 68
  dating methods of, 33–35
  excavations at Stonehenge
    by Atkinson, 32–33, 46
    by Cunnington, 30
    by Evans, 39
    by Gowland, 31
    by Hawley, 31–32, 39
    by Newall, 31, 39
    by Petrie, 33
    by Piggott, 32
    by Stone, 32
    by Stukeley, 15
  lessons from, 32
  methods of, 29, 30–31
Atkinson, Richard
  discovers carvings, 46
  on dressing of stones, 27
  on Great Trilithon, 48
  Heel Stone and, 38
  on phases of building Stone-henge, 32–33, 45
  on preservation of Stone-henge, 80
  on purpose of Stonehenge, 60
  restoration and, 80
  on Slaughter Stone, 56–57
  on Stonehenge Decoded, 71
  on stones of Stonehenge, 20–21
  on terrain during Neolithic period, 13
  on transportation of sarsens to Stonehenge, 26
Atlantis, 63
Aubrey, John
  discovers Aubrey holes, 39
  on Druids as builders of Stonehenge, 63, 64
  on folkore about Stonehenge, 77
  Heel Stone and, 38–39
  on human destruction of Stonehenge, 77
Aubrey holes, 39, 40
  astronomical purpose of, 70, 71, 72
  as markers, 47
Aurelius Ambrosius, 61, 62
Avebury circle, 15, 25
Avenue, 41–42, 56
  Stonehenge IV and, 59

barrows, 16–19, 24, 42, 66
baseline samples, 35
Beaker Folk, 40–41, 42–43, 45
bluestones
  as calendar, 69
  dressing of, 27
  origins of, 62
  source of, 21–22, 23–24
  Stonehenge II and, 42–43, 45, 46
  Stonehenge IIIb and, 57–58
  Stonehenge IIIc and, 58–59
  transported to Stonehenge, 22–23
  types of, 19
Bronze Age, 17
Buckingham, duke of, 65
burial customs, 17–19, 30–31
burial pits, 16–17
  Aubrey holes as, 39, 40
  see also barrows
Burl, Aubrey
  on effect of Stonehenge, 51
  on ley-lines, 67
Bush Barrow, 18–19

carbon dating. See radiocarbon dating
Carmenyn, 22
Castleden, Rodney
  on Carmenyn, 22
  on carvings at Stonehenge, 46–47

causeway, 37
Chippindale, Christopher, 72
Chubb, Cecil, 73
circles, ceremonial, 13–15
comparison dating, 35
Crampton, Patrick
  on Mount Prescelly, 23
Cunnington, William
  on barrows, 17
  on discoveries at Stonehenge,
    30
cursus, 15–16

Danes, 63
Devizes Museum, 18
Discover magazine, 75
dolerite, 19
dowsing, 67–68
Druids
  ancient, 63–64
  as described by Pliny the El-
    der, 68–69
  modern, 64–65, 81, 82–83
Durrington Walls, 14–15, 40

Earth Mysteries, 67
eclipses, lunar, 70–71
English Heritage Foundation
  as guardian, 9, 73–74
  preservation measures taken
    by, 81, 83
  preservation proposals of, 84,
    85
  virtual reality model of, 84–85
Enigma of Stonehenge, The
  (Fowles), 32, 75
entasis, 28
Evans, Arthur, 80
Evans, John, 39
extraterrestrials, 66

Foamhenge, 84
Fowles, John
  on archaeological discover-
    ies, 32
  on condition of Stonehenge, 75
  on impact of/reaction to
    Stonehenge, 85
  on tourists, 83

Garden of Eden, 66
Geoffrey of Monmouth, 60–62
Giants' Dance, 61
glaciers, 24
Gowland, William, 31, 80
graffiti, 78
graves. *See* barrows; burial pits
Great Cursus, 15–16
Great Trilithon, 48, 50, 56–57
Greeks, 63

Hawkes, Jacquetta, 72
Hawkins, Gerald, 69–71
Hawley, William, 31–32, 39
"Heart's Journey, The" (Sas-
  soon), 61
Heel Stone, 38–39
  bluestone circles and, 42
  lunar eclipses and, 71
henges, 14, 15
Henry of Huntingdon, 8–9
highways, 79, 84
Historia naturalis (Pliny the El-
  der), 68–69
Histories of the Kings of Britain
  (Geoffrey of Monmouth),
  60–62
Hoare, Richard Colt, 17
Hopkins, Roger, 26, 57
Hoyle, Fred, 69, 71
human sacrifices, 30–31

Intel, 84–85
Internet, 84–85
Ireland, 61, 62

James I, 62
Jones, Inigo, 62–63

Killaraus, Mount, 61

Leman, Thomas, 30–31
ley-lines, 67, 68
lintels, 14, 53–55
  from Avebury circle, 25
  bluestones as, 43
  restoration of, 80
  size of, 20–21

trilithons and, 27, 48
lunar eclipses, 70–71

Making of Stonehenge, The
  (Castleden), 46–47
Maranto, Gina, 75
Marborough Downs, 25, 45
Martin, Benjamin, 77
Merlin, 60–62
Mesolithic period, 12
Michell, John, 66
military bases, 79, 84
Millennium Park, 85
mounds, burial. *See* barrows;
  burial pits

National Trust
  as owner of Stonehenge, 9,
    73–74
  preservation measures taken
    by, 81, 83
  preservation proposals of, 84
Neolithic period, 12–13, 15, 24,
  36
Newall, Robert, 31, 39
Normanton Down, 17–18

Old Stone Age, 12

People's Free Festival, 79, 81, 82
Petrie, Sir Flinders, 33, 35
Phoenicians, 63
Piggott, Stuart, 32, 80
Pliny the Elder, 63, 68–69
pollution, 79
Prescelly, Mount, 22
Public Order Act (1986), 82–83

Q holes, 43

radiocarbon dating, 33–35, 59,
  71
R holes, 43
rhyolite, 19
Richards, Julian, 57
Robin Hood's Ball, 13–14
Robinson, Paul, 18
Romans, 30, 62–63, 65, 76

Salisbury Plain, 8, 17, 75
sandstone, 19–20, 44
sarsens
  as calendar, 69, 70
  choice of, 25
  described, 19–20
  dressing of, 27–28
  graffiti on, 78
  Heel Stone and, 38
  restoration of, 80
  size of, 20–21
  source of, 25
  as Station Stones, 40
  Stonehenge IIIa and, 45–46,
    46–49, 53
  Stonehenge IIIc and, 58–59
  transported to Stonehenge,
    25–26
Sassoon, Siegfried, 61
Sebastian, Tim, 65
"Secrets of Lost Empires, The"
  (film), 56–57
sequence dating, 35
Slaughter Stone, 56
stanenges, 8–9
Station Stones, 42, 47
Stone, J. F. S., 32
Stone Age, 12, 17
Stonehenge
  abandonment of, 39–40
  builders of, 13, 56
  construction of, 10
    dressing of stones, 27–28,
      45–46
    materials used. *See* blue-
      stones; sarsens
    methods used, 49–51,
      53–55
    tools used, 27, 31, 36
  dating of, 33, 35
  described, 8–9, 51, 85
  destruction of, 74
    by humans, 76–79
    by weather, 75
  legends about, 19, 63, 77
    Druids and, 63–65
    Elizabethan, 38–39
    Merlin and, 60–62

Romans and, 62–63
location of, 11
military bases and, 79, 84
ownership of, 73–74
phase I, 33
    Aubrey holes, 39
    causeway, 37
    construction of, 35–37
    Heel Stone, 38–39
    Station Stones, 40
phase II, 33
    Altar Stone, 44
    Avenue, 41–42
    Beaker Folk and, 40–41,
        42–43
    bluestone circles, 42–43,
        45, 46
    Station Stones, 40, 42
phase IIIa, 33
    Aubrey holes, 47
    lintels, 53–55
    sarsens, 45–47, 53
    Slaughter Stone, 56
    Station Stones, 47
    trilithons, 47–48
phase IIIb, 33, 57–58
phase IIIc, 33, 58–59
phase IV, 33, 42, 59
preservation of
    measures taken, 80–83
    proposals for, 83–84
purpose of, 11, 44, 48, 60
    astronomical, 69–72
    religious, 72
restoration of, 79–80
Stonehenge (Atkinson), 20–21
"Stonehenge: Can It Be
    Saved?" (Maranto), 75
Stonehenge Decoded
    (Hawkins), 69–71
Stonehenge of the Kings
    (Crampton), 23

Stonehenge People, The (Burl),
    51
Stukeley, William, 77–78
    Druid theory and, 64
    on effect of Stonehenge, 51
    Great Cursus and, 15
summer solstice, 81, 82–83
    Beaker Folk and, 41
    causeway and, 37
    Druids and, 64–65
    Heel Stone and, 38
    Station Stones and, 40
    Stonehenge and, 33

Templa Druidum (Aubrey), 63,
    64
Times (London), 29
tools, 27, 31, 36
tourists, 9, 75, 76–77, 81, 82, 83
trilithons
    dressing of, 27
    restoration of, 80
    Stonehenge IIIa and, 47–48
    Stonehenge IIIb and, 57

Wales, 22, 44
Washington, Lawrence, 73
Watkins, Alfred, 67
weather, 75
Wessex people, 45
Whitby, Mark
    on builders of Stonehenge, 56
    on construction methods, 55
    on transportation of sarsens
        to Stonehenge, 25–26
William of Newburg, 62
Wiltshire, 8, 11
Woodhenge, 14, 32, 40
World Heritage Sites, 73

Y holes, 58

Z holes, 58

PICTURE CREDITS

ABOUT THE AUTHOR

Wendy Mass holds a B.A. in English from Tufts University and an M.A. in creative writing from California State University, Long Beach. She is the cofounder and editor of a national literary journal for teenagers called *Writes of Passage* and is the author of fiction and nonfiction books and articles for young adults. She has worked as a book editor for Longmeadow Press and Reader's Digest Young Families and currently lives in San Francisco. Ms. Mass has written three books for Lucent Books.